Unforgettable
NEW JERSEY
Characters

UNFORGETTABLE NEW JERSEY CHARACTERS

Heroes, Scoundrels, Politicians and More

Joseph Bilby and Harry Ziegler

THE
History
PRESS

Published by The History Press
Charleston, SC
www.historypress.com

First published 2022

Manufactured in the United States

ISBN 9781467146838

Library of Congress Control Number: 2022935417

This book is dedicated to the memory of Nurse Cornelia Hancock, Private Alexander Springsteen, Corporal Charles Hopkins, Sergeant George Ashby, Sergeant John Basilone, Major William Reddan, Colonel Ruth Cheney Streeter, General Donald McGowan and all New Jerseyans who have served their state and country faithfully and honorably in times of war, from the War for Independence to the current day, and continued to do so in peace.

CONTENTS

ACKNOWLEDGEMENTS

No author of a nonfiction book can go it alone, so we would particularly like to thank John J. McGowan, the Reddan family, Monmouth University professor Melissa Ziobro, NGMMNJ curator and Staff Sergeant Andrew Walker and Assistant Curator Carol Fowler.

INTRODUCTION

They were famous or infamous or had a flash of state and/or national recognition in their day, and some of their stories were widely known in the state and even around the country. But fame is, as they say, fleeting, and often infamy, less likely to fade, is as well. This book will be composed of brief biographies of once notable New Jerseyans between the years 1775 and 1950 whom time has forgotten.

The subjects include a city treasurer who ran away to Mexico with the city's money and a dancing girl from New York; the first big-time lobbyist, who was shot in his mistress's bedroom; a governor who ended up in a county jail; the man credited with founding Labor Day; the first woman mayor in the state; the first woman elected to Congress from the state; a Communist-chasing congressman who ended up in prison; a freelance hangman; a religious lady who founded a church and supported the Ku Klux Klan; the last Civil War veteran; and many, many more.

SAMUEL ALLEN

Hero, Scoundrel or Fictional Character?

H e was considered a hero by his descendants and the public in 1923, but today he might well be considered a scoundrel. And there is also the question of his very existence. If you drive down Route 70 toward the Manasquan River in New Jersey and glance to your right where a small stone monument stands, barely visible alongside the road, and if you are interested in history, you might be inclined to stop and read the plaque on the stone, which is revealing…and a bit bizarre.

Monmouth County, New Jersey, was torn by internal strife during the Revolution, with atrocities on both sides, most notably the lynching of Captain Joshua Huddy by Loyalists seeking revenge for the apparent murder of Tory Philip White, who was killed by Patriot militiamen "while trying to escape" on the way to Freehold. The "Associated Loyalists" led by William Franklin, former royal governor and the son of Benjamin Franklin, gave rise to the Association for Purposes of Retaliation, a Patriot organization intended to combat both Loyalist raiders and their local sympathizers. The group's charter, "The Articles of Association for Purposes of Retaliation," is a document that clearly exemplifies the principle of an "eye for an eye."

Due to this internecine struggle, which went on even after the end of actual large-scale hostilities with the American victory at Yorktown, there seems to have been little enthusiasm in Monmouth County to commemorate the conflict—or even the massive and significant battle of Monmouth Court House in its aftermath. An 1846 attempt to raise money to erect a six-foot-tall Italian marble obelisk on the site of the crucial battle failed to garner the required funds. The current monument was not dedicated until 1884, due to the efforts of former governor Joel Parker.

Memorialization of all sorts gathered momentum in the late nineteenth and early twentieth centuries, and the plaque on the stone alongside Route 70 was an example of this awakened interest in history, or what was believed to be history. In 1927, the Daughters of the American Revolution and the descendants of a Captain Samuel Allen placed the plaque, which reads, "To perpetuate the memory of CAPT. SAMUEL ALLEN, organizer and leader of a regiment of volunteer Minute Men of the New Jersey Coast during the Revolutionary War, 1775–1783. This stone marks the spot where Capt. Allen executed six Tories and their chief"—presumably on his own authority without benefit of trial, in what would be classified today as a lynching.

The dedication was quite an affair, attended by a considerable crowd. An army band from Fort Monmouth played "America" to open the ceremony, followed by Reverend James E. Shaw of the Spring Lake Methodist Episcopal Church's invocation. Eight boys and girls then presented "the evolution of the flag" and led a recitation of the Pledge of Allegiance. Mrs. Edgar Braley of Spring Lake sang "a patriotic solo," and then Addison Allen of Yonkers, New York, "a great grandson of Captain Allen, read a history of the captain's heroic deeds"; the captain's "only surviving grandson," Theodore Allen of Brooklyn, laid a wreath on the monument.

New Jersey governor A. Harry Moore gave the major address, praising patriotism and obliquely referring to the lynching, saying, "We do not rejoice in that. We like to emphasize the reason he hanged them. The ideals that actuated him to do it." The ceremony ended with a benediction by Reverend Shaw and a salute fired by members of Troop B of the 102nd Cavalry Regiment, a New Jersey National Guard unit from Red Bank.

Despite all the praise, who Captain Samuel Allen was or even if he existed at all is more than a bit murky. As a captain, he would not have been a regimental commander, as that position was held by a colonel. A search of New Jersey Revolutionary War service records turned up several men of the same name, but none in the Monmouth County militia. In 1971, a reporter from the *Asbury Park Press* took a close look at the Allen story, noting that an amateur history of Wall Township published in 1965 claimed that the captain was a cousin of Ethan Allen and asserted that he had been captured four times by Tories, who burned his farm; he escaped each time and caught the perpetrators, allegedly led by a "Captain Tighe," following the fourth attack and hanged them in revenge. The vague reference to "Tighe" was likely based on the activities of Titus or "Colonel Tye." Titus was a former

Samuel Allen monument. *Author's collection.*

slave of John Corlies of Shrewsbury who escaped and joined the Loyalist guerrillas headquartered on Sandy Hook. Tye led a number of raids into Monmouth County until he was mortally wounded.

The author of the "history" took the information he dispensed on the Allen family from a 1959 article on Allen in the *Red Bank Register*. The *Register* used, as its source, an article "that was published in the *Journal of American History* about forty years ago." The author of that article was cited as "Colonel Ethan Allen, a grandson of Capt. Samuel Allen, who was a recruiting colonel for the Union army during the Civil War and who was president of the Cuban League during the Spanish American war." In fact, a survey of data shows no one named Ethan Allen who served in the Union army above the rank of corporal, although he may have served in a state militia organization. A "Colonel Ethan Allen" of New York was a leading officer in the Cuban League, an organization founded to advocate for the Cuban rebellion against Spain over Cuba.

The article by Colonel Ethan Allen describes Samuel as "a bold dashing daredevil, a boy not yet of age at the opening of the war, of commanding influence because of his wealth and his overbearing will, he was, while the conflict lasted, the General-in-chief of all Military movements pertaining to his district and the sole judge of all prisoners brought before him," presumably an excuse for his being able to lynch prisoners.

There is absolutely no evidence to confirm any of these stories and no mention of the alleged incident in newspapers of the era, which reported even minor actions between Tories and Patriots. The only reference to a Samuel Allen in Monmouth County the reporter could find was as a claimant in an Allentown disposition of loot from a privateering voyage. Most tellingly, Samuel Allen's name does not appear among the signers of "The Articles of Association for Purposes of Retaliation," which was signed by the most aggressive Patriots in the county. A roster of the people of Monmouth County during the Revolutionary era lists a Samuel Allen in Shrewsbury who was "indicted for misdemeanor" twice in 1782 and a Samuel Allen Jr., probably the son of the indicted Allen, from Shrewsbury, who served as a private in the Continental army, and no other men with that name.

So, who was Captain Samuel Allen? Was he a hero or a scoundrel...or did he not even exist? The mystery continues, but the likely conclusion is the third option.

DAVID FORMAN

Patriot or Devil

The election of David Forman to the chairmanship led to a split between the more restrained and the more active members of the Association for Purposes of Retaliation, a group that was created to oppose Tory raiders into Monmouth County. He had been stripped of his militia rank (he retained a commission as a colonel in the Continental army) by the state legislature over accusations of rigging elections, plundering suspected Tories without proof of any wrongdoing and prizing his own economic interest above other concerns. Several of Forman's relatives and associates held positions of significant power within the county, including sheriff, justices of the peace, judges and officers in both the Continental army and the county militia. Forman, known by those who incurred his wrath as "Black David" and "Devil Dave," the former due to his "swarthy complexion," was himself a judge for both the Court of Oyer and Terminer and the Court of Common Pleas during the Revolutionary War era.

Forman, who appeared during the opening phase of the 1778 battle at Freehold Court House only to fade from view once the action got hot, was known to turn his various titles to his own personal advantage whenever possible. One famous instance had to do with the Union Salt Works on the Manasquan River in what is now Brielle, in which Forman had a personal fiscal stake. While the Battles of Trenton and Princeton raged in late December 1776 and early January 1777, Forman declined to join in the action, preferring to use soldiers under his command to work at and guard his salt works. Salt was an extremely important strategic commodity in the

David Forman. *Courtesy of Wikimedia Commons.*

eighteenth century, used in the preservation of meat. In October 1776, the New Jersey legislature encouraged private individuals to erect salt making establishments along the coast, distilling the product from ocean water, and a year later planned for a state-owned salt works. The latter idea was abandoned when it became clear that private efforts would suffice.

Although General Washington at first consented to this use of the troops at the salt works, assured as he was by Forman that he would soon be producing salt for military consumption, it was soon revealed that troops for a Continental army regiment he was authorized to recruit were also busy building the works for Forman's personal for-profit enterprise. In this role, they provided free labor for Forman but were of little advantage to an army that needed them. Following an investigation by the state Council of Safety, Washington requested the troops be reassigned to the main army, although some apparently remained in Forman's employ up to seven months later.

Forman thus brought extensive baggage with him to the chairmanship of the Association for Purposes of Retaliation. He was, however, also charismatic and well connected. The Retaliators likely sought to gain status and clout from Forman's position in the local establishment, but his soured relationship with the state legislature doomed the association to remain an extra-legal organization. Furthermore, Forman's polarizing effect eventually drove off many moderate Retaliators, who were genuinely interested in self-defense, creating a group more focused on aggression and plunder than ever before.

The Retaliators continued to play a double game, simultaneously petitioning the New Jersey legislature for recognition while carrying out unapproved vigilantism behind its back. In September 1780, the legislature convened a committee to examine the situation in Monmouth County and consider the petitions of the association. Its final report recognized the vulnerability of the county to Tory raids and recommended that more militia and semi-regular state troops be assigned to active duty in the area. The committee did not view the Association for Purposes of Retaliation as making a positive contribution to local security. The report condemned the Retaliators as a subversive, terroristic group and advised that Loyalist plunderers were most effectively dealt with through legal channels. The legislature stopped short, however, of explicitly banning the group. Its members likely recognized its inability to enforce a moratorium of the association's activities.

After the war, Forman moved to Chestertown, Maryland, and then later to Natchez, Mississippi, where he purchased a plantation and its slave labor force. One account from the *Asbury Park Press* in 1949 notes that he was then "seized with apoplexy, sought to get to New York from New Orleans on a boat, was captured in the Gulf of Mexico by a British privateer, then taken to the Bahamas where General Forman died Sept. 12, 1799, at the age of 52."

In the years following the Revolution, Monmouth County tried to forget its troubled times during the conflict. Although Forman was recalled by some as a "well remembered hero," there is a story, though, that local mothers used to threaten their children that if their behavior did not improve, "Devil Dave" would get them. In 1876, a minister marking veteran graves with flags failed to post one on Forman's grave site, explaining that he ran out of flags. Perhaps.

By 1899, however, "Devil Dave" had become somewhat rehabilitated through the work of a family descendant, Mrs. Althea Weathersby of Trenton. She presented a talk on Forman that was described as "very flowery in its passages and it detailed at length the deeds of the old hero." Was it an accurate account? You decide.

SAM PATCH

The "Jersey Jumper"

In the early nineteenth century, spectator sports were a rarity, which meant a "jumper" could become a celebrity. On September 30, 1827, twenty-year-old Sam Patch—an employee of Paterson, New Jersey's Hamilton Mills cotton factory—jumped off a cliff into the Passaic River near the newly built bridge over the Paterson falls. Patch survived the eighty-foot drop and swam to shore. In succeeding days, he repeated the feat several times, passing a hat around the crowd afterward. It was the beginning of a brief but spectacular career as a risk-taking entrepreneur and an "indigenous folk hero."

Born and raised in Pawtucket, Rhode Island, Patch, as was common at the time, went to work as a child in a cotton mill. Before moving to Paterson, he had established a minor local reputation as a "jumper" and had steadily increased the risks of his stunts until his dive into the Passaic. Following his series of Paterson jumps, Patch hurled himself some ninety feet off a ship mast into the Hudson River at Hoboken. Bored with the monotonous work and poor pay of a "cotton spinner" in a Paterson mill, he became a full-time professional daredevil, known far and wide as the "Jersey Jumper" and an "aero-nautical performer," who accomplished a series of feats across the Northeast, allegedly tossing a pet bear into the water before jumping himself. A much-cited Patch quote, albeit puzzling to today's reader, was: "Some things can be done as well as others." Another "Patchism" was "There's no mistake in Sam Patch."

In October 1828, Patch made several 130-foot jumps over Niagara Falls, and on Friday, November 13, 1829, he made his final leap. Before a crowd

A nineteenth-century artist's version of a Sam Patch jump. *Author's collection.*

of about ten thousand curious Americans and Canadians at Genesee Falls, New York, Patch jumped off a ledge 125 feet above the Genesee River. After hitting the water, he failed to surface. One version of the end of the story reports that Sam's body was recovered several days later, while another, more reliable account notes that in March 1830, a local farmer discovered the Jersey Jumper's frozen remains under river ice several miles from where he jumped four months earlier. Patch's pauper's grave marker, a simple wooden plank in Charlotte Cemetery, was inscribed, "Here lies Sam Patch, such is Fame."

Author Nathaniel Hawthorne visited the grave and wrote:

> *How stern a moral may be drawn from the story of Poor Sam Patch. Why do we call him a madman or a fool when he has left his memory around the falls of the Genesee, more permanently than if the letters of his name had been hewn into the forehead of the precipice? Was the leaper of cataracts more mad or foolish than other men who throw away life or misspend it in pursuit of empty fame, and seldom so triumphantly as he? That which he won is as invaluable as any, except the unsought glory, spreading, like the rich perfume of richer fruit, from virtuous and useful deeds.*

Conspiracy theories and alleged hoaxes always sell, and shortly after his demise, a letter signed "Sam Patch of New Jersey" appeared in the *Boston*

Traveler and *New York Evening Post* newspapers alleging that he was "alive and kicking." He was, unfortunately, not. Patch's fame persisted for a few years in several traveling plays based on his career, and then the "Jersey Jumper" faded into the mists of history. His grave marker rotted away, but a group of local high school students raised money for a replacement stone marker in the mid-twentieth century. It still stands.

Sam made a postmortem appearance in a 1981 novel in which he travels with a bear in "a picaresque adventure, an early American tall tale and social satire." He would no doubt have been amused.

CORNELIA HANCOCK

America's Florence Nightingale

Cornelia Hancock, who would become known as the "Florence Nightingale of America," was born on February 6, 1840, to an old New Jersey Quaker family at Hancock's Bridge in Salem County. Hancock was introduced to social work through her brother-in-law, a Philadelphia physician.

As a result of the large numbers of casualties at the Battle of Gettysburg in July 1863, the military requested civilian medical assistance. Hancock's brother-in-law answered the call and took her with him, despite the disapproving orders of Superintendent of Nurses Dorothea Dix, who thought Cornelia unsuitable for nursing soldiers because she was too young and attractive. Hancock arrived at Gettysburg two days after the battle and without any official support or supplies, but she helped wherever she could, writing letters for the wounded, praying with them, making them comfortable with blankets and foraging for food supplies. Despite her innate dislike of alcohol, she dispensed it with scruples and began to serve what would become a trademark "punch" of condensed milk laced with whiskey.

In addition to her material aid, Hancock's cheery mood and optimism did much to raise the morale of her patients, and she quickly became an indispensable army nurse, serving through the winter camp of 1863–64 and the brutal Overland Campaign of the spring of 1864. Cornelia Hancock was one of the first Union women to enter Richmond after its capture. Although she was particularly highly regarded among the South Jersey men of the 12th New Jersey Infantry, soldiers throughout the Army of the

Left: Cornelia Hancock in 1860. *Author's collection.*

Right: Cornelia Hancock at the 1913 Gettysburg reunion (*second from left*). *Courtesy of the Hancock House.*

Potomac recognized and cheered her whenever she appeared. A dance tune, "The Hancock Gallop," was written in her honor, and a medal was cast to commemorate her service.

After the war, Hancock, supported by other Quakers, moved to South Carolina and founded a school for formerly enslaved children that eventually reached an enrollment of several hundred students. After leaving the South for health reasons in 1875, she spent much of the rest of her life in social work in Philadelphia and was especially active and successful in Wrightsville, a poverty-stricken neighborhood in the southwest section of the city.

As the nineteenth century waned, a newspaper noted about Hancock that "few of those she is likely to meet perhaps are aware of the mark that this lady has made on the history of this country by her assiduous attentions to the wounded on the battlefield of the late war. She was one of the most zealous and untiring women who ministered to the wounded at the front."

Hancock attended several reunions of the 12th New Jersey Infantry, and at the 1907 affair, a newspaper noted that she was wearing a watch chain that had her medal attached to it. The medal was inscribed on one side, "Miss Cornelia Hancock, Salem, New Jersey. Presented by the wounded soldiers, 3rd Division, Second Army Corps." On the other side was written, "Testimonial of regard for ministrations of mercy to the wounded soldiers at Gettysburg, PA. in July 1863."

Lauded for her war work at the reunion, Hancock was asked to give a speech. She rose and said, "I am not a talker. I am a doer." She received a large round of applause, which left her in tears.

Hancock was also present, along with other nurses, at the 1913 fiftieth anniversary reunion at Gettysburg. Cornelia Hancock died from nephritis on December 31, 1927, at her home in Atlantic City and was buried at Harmersville.

OLIVER HALSTED

Newark's Lobbyist and Lover

The Civil War submarine dubbed the "Intelligent Whale" was invented by Scoville Merriam of Massachusetts. In November 1863, a group of New Jersey investors led by William Halsted, former commander of the 1st New Jersey Cavalry, funded the construction of the vessel. The Whale had a door in the bottom that could be opened to allow a diver to leave the submarine to remove obstructions or plant mines. The air pressure in the submarine exceeded the outside water pressure, thus allowing the diver to leave and return without the craft flooding.

Newark attorney Oliver S. "Pet" Halsted, a relative of William's, had moved to Long Branch in the summer of 1861 when he learned that Mary Lincoln was spending the summer there. He joined her entourage when she left for Washington and became the first big-time lobbyist. If you wanted to sell something to the Union army or navy, you hired Oliver. The owners of the Whale hired him to represent them to sell the submarine to the navy, and it was tested in Long Island Sound in August 1864, when it successfully submerged and then returned to the surface. The navy declined to purchase it due to fears regarding its seaworthiness, even after a more comprehensive test report in the October 1864 issue of *Scientific American* magazine noted that "in all respects the vessel worked so completely that its success is undoubted."

Stymied by the failure of his sales pitch, Halsted eventually bought the submarine himself and, in 1866, tried to sell it to the Fenians, the American branch of the Irish Republican Brotherhood. The organization was more interested in a submarine that could sink British ships, however, and declined to purchase the Whale. Halsted finally managed to convince the Union navy to buy it, though at a discount. Transported to the Brooklyn Navy Yard, the Intelligent Whale was unsuccessfully tested there several years later.

Oliver Halsted. *Author's collection.*

It was suggested that the navy contact Halsted for assistance, but he was no longer available. The fifty-two-year-old Halsted had a large family in Newark, but he also had a mistress, thirty-seven-year-old Mary Wilson, whom he had installed in an apartment above a saloon at 95 South Street in the city, not far from his "handsome residence" at Parkhurst and South Broad Streets. With his family on vacation on Long Island, Halsted took the opportunity to spend the night with Ms. Wilson, described as "a lady of prepossessing appearance."

Unfortunately for Halsted, George Botts, a "charcoal peddler" and another intimate friend of the "disreputable woman," who had more than a few drinks, caught him in the apartment in bed with Wilson at 7:30 a.m. on July 2, 1871; after a "brief struggle," Botts drew a revolver and shot Halsted dead. A newspaper account of his demise characterized Halsted as a "public celebrity, his name and actions being household words not alone in New Jersey but across the Union." Mary Wilson, who was described as someone whom "others, well known in Newark, have also had associations with," was arrested as a material witness. Not to be outdone by twentieth-century tabloids, the *Newark Daily Advertiser* headlined the incident "Shocking Results of Guilty Love, Jealousy, Rum and Passion."

Botts was arrested shortly afterward and allegedly told the arresting officers that although he might spend the Fourth of July in jail, Halsted would spend it in a "worse place." Botts was headed for the same place as well and was quickly tried and convicted of Halsted's murder. He was hanged in Newark in January 1872 and made the papers again in a detailed account of his execution, in which he was hoisted up by the noose rather than dropped through a gallows trapdoor.

The Intelligent Whale on display at the National Guard Militia Museum of New Jersey. *Courtesy of Spec4 Michael Schwenkert, DMAVA Public Affairs.*

The Intelligent Whale ended up as an ornament on the Brooklyn Navy Yard commander's lawn. When that navy yard closed, the submarine was shipped to the Washington Navy Yard. It remained there until it returned to New Jersey in 1999, and it currently resides at the National Guard Militia Museum of New Jersey in Sea Girt. It is the only surviving Union Civil War submarine and a major attraction at the museum, as well as the only surviving artifact of Oliver Halsted's once famed career. The site of his "large and elegant mansion" is now occupied by a Dunkin' Donuts shop.

WILLIE McGEE

Drummer Boy

From a Medal of Honor recipient at the age of fifteen to a street derelict who killed another man over beef stew, William Henry "Willie" McGee enjoyed a brief blaze of glory before descending into a life marred by alcohol and violence. Hailed in his early years as a "gallant young hero," McGee became the object of scorn and derision after a series of personal blunders and, ultimately, the disclosure that he was not deserving of his medal.

His life began inauspiciously enough. McGee was born on May 13, 1849, in Newark, New Jersey, the son of Irish immigrants. In 1855, McGee's father died, and by 1860, McGee was living with an aunt and uncle in the city.

McGee's life underwent a dramatic change in 1863, when he left his job as a waiter to enlist in the 33rd New Jersey Infantry's Company C as a musician. He appears to have campaigned with the regiment through January 1864, when he was hospitalized with typhoid and met his first of several enthusiastic supporters, Holmes Pattison.

Pattison, who served as chaplain at Murfreesboro Hospital, encountered young McGee when he arrived with other sick and wounded members of his unit. McGee "must have presented a very forlorn figure," according to a newspaper account. "Though he listed himself as 5' 2" upon entering the service in Newark, to an observer, McGee, sickly, thin, and possessing a boyishly haggard Irish countenance, might easily have been passed for eleven or twelve when he was carried into Hospital #2 at Murfreesboro."

As his health improved, McGee began to showcase his magnetic personality, cultivating a friendship with Pattison. "By all accounts Willie was a most intrinsically gregarious charmer, and as he returned to health, the Reverend Pattison, an attorney by trade, for whatever reasons, felt his heart tug and legally adopted the young drummer boy," according to a local newspaper. Certainly, the adoption was an unorthodox one, since McGee was not an orphan and openly admitted that he had a large extended family in Newark. Nevertheless, within a few months of meeting, Pattison adopted the fifteen-year-old and became a staunch advocate for the youth until a falling-out in 1872.

Following his recovery, McGee embarked on a military adventure that would earn him a place in history. In December 1864, serving as a mounted orderly during a small battle in the Nashville campaign, McGee reportedly rallied two regiments and led them to capture enemy artillery and several hundred prisoners. He was awarded the Medal of Honor for his actions.

As a journalist noted, "It was no ordinary victory, but the turning point of the crisis, and the series of quickly succeeding battles that finally drove [Confederate General John Bell] Hood from Tennessee." News accounts of the time hailed McGee as a gallant young hero whose story was "so much like the romances of the days of knightly exploit."

After the close of the war, McGee was appointed a second lieutenant in the 20th U.S. Infantry but lacked the educational background to pass the scrutiny of the examining board. Ever the gregarious networker, McGee enlisted the aid of his adopted "father," Pattison, who persuaded Governor Marcus Ward of New Jersey to hire tutors for the ambitious young soldier.

The investment paid off: "[A]pplying himself to the books with the same intelligence and indomitable pluck that marked his conduct in the field, [McGee] was soon ready to appear again before the examining board and this time passed triumphantly."

The little drummer boy from Newark had risen to great heights at a remarkably young age, but his descent was to be equally swift and dramatic. "Little Willie McGee could grow old and happy with what he had already accomplished, but such was not to be his fate," wrote Thomas Fox in a biography of the unlucky young soldier. An increasing dependence on alcohol undoubtedly played a key role in a series of personal blunders.

While stationed with his regiment at Baton Rouge, McGee was accused by the unit's assistant surgeon of stealing his watch. "It was the first blur which had ever been cast upon his honor," a newspaper stated. "In a moment of anger, he visited the quarters of the Surgeon and demanded retraction. When the physician refused, an enraged McGee struck him with a cowhide. The doctor reached for his nearby weapon, but McGee was quicker, firing a fatal gunshot." The tragedy created a stir in the city, as noted by the Baton Rouge *Tri-Weekly Advocate*: "Both officers having many warm friends in this city, great regret for the occurrence is expressed and much sympathy felt, for both the living and the dead, who were parties to this unfortunate affair."

McGee was tried for manslaughter by a civil court and acquitted. It is highly likely, however, that when he was freed "he was placed under rearrest and sent to the brig," according to Fox, his biographer. The U.S. Army convened a court-martial to show "its own special definition of honor and justice." The verdict: five years in prison. Ironically, General E.D. Townsend, the same adjutant general who signed McGee's Medal of Honor application three years

Willie McGee as an army lieutenant. *Courtesy of Thomas Fox.*

before, approved and signed McGee's court-martial papers on April 9, 1869.

McGee ended up in federal prison in dreary Stillwater, Minnesota. "Entering his cell, William McGee could be forgiven if he shuddered at more than the Minnesota weather," observed Fox. Clad in his standard-issue striped "zebra suit," McGee arose at 5:30 a.m. each day and labored at his assigned workplace for twelve hours. Dinner was eaten in silence before McGee reported to his tiny cell. Rules were strict—no laughing, talking at work or staring at visitors—and heavily enforced.

Once again, however, McGee's charm and connections saved the day. Former governor Marcus Ward, an admirer of McGee's since his halcyon days as a Medal of Honor recipient, successfully lobbied to win a pardon after little more than a year in prison. The *Newark Advertiser* proclaimed that, given the second chance, McGee would redeem himself: "[A]ll rejoice that the young man is now free to begin over again a career in which he has displayed such remarkable talent."

Unfortunately, McGee abandoned all efforts to restore the luster of his military career, instead drifting further into a life of drink and dissolution. After using Ward to receive a presidential pardon, McGee pawned his

Medal of Honor and then panhandled money from Ward to retrieve it. He married three different women and deserted them, joined the 7th U.S. Cavalry as an enlisted man and later passed himself off as the only survivor of Custer's Last Stand.

In 1878, after a stint as a hobo, McGee applied for a disability pension, a move that would prove disastrous. To document McGee's heroism, which garnered him the Medal of Honor, McGee's lawyer contacted retired general Horatio Van Cleve, who allegedly entrusted McGee with the troops that the drummer boy led to victory on that fateful day in 1864. Unfortunately, Van Cleve wrote, it never happened: "He knows well that he was never wounded while acting as an orderly for me and he also knows that the story circulated some years ago of his capturing a rebel battery while he was acting under my orders—he knows is a sheer fabrication of his brain." The revelation, noted biographer Fox, was a catastrophic development for the ill-fated McGee: "McGee's reputation in New Jersey, already damaged due to his imprisonment and alcohol abuse, was dealt a fatal blow with Van Cleve's letter."

The years that followed were grim, culminating in a murder over a quarrel about the proper preparation of beef stew. "Beef Stew Causes Tragedy" trumpeted the *New York Times* headline on December 12, 1904. McGee was charged with the stabbing murder of his friend, salesman Frank Mitchell, after the two engaged in a heated argument over the best way to cook a stew. The fatal wound had penetrated seven inches, passing through Mitchell's stomach and cutting into his liver.

Sentenced to seven years and ten months for the murder, McGee was registered as an inmate in the notorious Sing Sing Prison, thirty miles upriver from New York City. Historian Timothy J. Gilfoyle compared the jail to a Soviet gulag, rife with "[t]orture, disease, insanity, injury and death." Prison records from the era no longer exist, so McGee's fate and resting place are unknown.

In the end, McGee's life was a troubled tale of unmet potential and broken dreams. As biographer Thomas Fox concluded, McGee was "another precocious boy who went to war too soon in a world where no one cared how old you were; a displaced spirit who wove a life behind the cloak of lies and a brilliant, hypnotic personality; a son of New Jersey never able to fondly embrace life; and a forgotten, broken man who fought demons and lost."

ALEXANDER D. HAMILTON

Jersey City's "Defaulter"

Another Defaulter," trumpeted the headline in the January 28, 1874 edition of the *Brooklyn Daily Eagle*. The article noted that Jersey City's treasurer, Alexander D. Hamilton, had decamped with $100,000 cash and $50,000 worth of city bonds. The inhabitants of that "quiet burgh" were thrown into a state of "great excitement" that Hamilton had taken a large portion of the city's funds, violating the municipal regulation that forbade the treasurer from leaving the city without the consent of the city's board of finance.

Instead, the errant city official disappeared on a Friday night, later telegraphing his family from Boston "saying that he had been obliged to go to that city on important business" but would return soon. Hamilton never did come home and, in fact, ran off with an attractive young actress, whom he abandoned in Philadelphia. His disappearance triggered a lengthy and arduous investigation that led to the wilds of Texas and a bandit's den in Mexico.

Prior to the Jersey City scandal, Hamilton's life was respectable enough. He was born in 1844 in Jersey City and enlisted as a sergeant in the 2nd New Jersey Cavalry in September 1863, promoted to second lieutenant and then first lieutenant in 1864 and discharged at Vicksburg, Mississippi, on November 1, 1865. The Jersey City debacle, however, marked a turn for the worse in the young man's life, which would be characterized by a series of outrageous misadventures in the years ahead.

Following his stop in Philadelphia, Hamilton headed to Texas, finally landing in Mexico living under the protection of Juan Cortina, the leader of "a powerful band of outlaws," according to news reports. Hot on the trail was Jersey City police sergeant Benjamin Murphy, who was sent there to capture him.

In later years, Hamilton regaled a reporter with his version of the journey west, no doubt riddled with exaggeration. His elaborate tale included the following highlights. Once in Texas, Hamilton employed a guide, Charles Hutchinson, who was accompanied by several Mexicans who "looked as if they would cut your throat for a dollar." According to Hamilton,

Alexander Hamilton. *Courtesy of Jim Madden.*

the group was accosted by the Corpus Christi police chief, who demanded $300 to allow Hamilton to continue his journey. Hamilton complied, but the police chief returned later that day with several henchmen, demanding more money.

"I was determined to fight for the money in my possession, and I cocked the carbine I had and told them I would shoot the first man that laid hands on me," Hamilton said. After realizing that his captors would murder him if he resisted, Hamilton gave them $17,000 in cash, keeping $42,000 in bonds, which the men did not want. Everyone left, including the tour guide, Hutchinson, leaving Hamilton with two Mexican guides.

Once Hamilton crossed the Rio Grande in a skiff and reached the haven of Matamoras, Mexico, he set up headquarters at Happy Jack's Hotel and sent for General Cortina, the town's mayor and a notorious outlaw known as the Red Robber of the Rio Grande. "I made a bargain with him," Hamilton recalled. "The nature of that transaction I refuse to divulge. He promised to protect me, however." Deducing that Cortina's protection would only last as long as Hamilton's money, Murphy, who had trailed the defaulter to Mexico, patiently waited "till the outlaw should turn the fugitive out from among them, penniless."

He did not wait long. Cortina robbed his ward of all he had and then abandoned him, allowing Murphy to apprehend the felon and return to Jersey City. Another version of the end of the story had Cortina putting Hamilton on a boat to Brazil but eventually making his way home and surrendering to Murphy in Jersey City.

Following his return, Hamilton's cavalier attitude toward his family resulted in bitterness and heartache. His loyal wife, Sarah, suffered the most, as reflected in her obituary published in the *New York Times* on June 5, 1881. Entitled "The Grand Qualities Shown by the Wife of a Rascal," the article said Mrs. Hamilton's life illustrated a "touching story of wifely devotion." When Hamilton was returned to Jersey City, the story noted, the first person to greet him was his wife, "who forgave him the disgrace he had brought upon her and her children."

The dutiful Mrs. Hamilton became an outspoken advocate for her husband, convincing the judge to impose a comparatively lenient sentence of three years' imprisonment. When Hamilton was released a year before his term would have expired, Mrs. Hamilton "placed the remnants of her little fortune in his hands and bade him make a new man of himself." At first, all was well. Hamilton's friends "believed that he was on the fair road to redemption, and all gave him a lifting hand." Hamilton established a milk route that employed three men and "yielded a handsome income."

Unfortunately, old habits slowly returned, and Hamilton "fell back into evil company." He sold the milk route and purchased a saloon, where he started a variety show of "the very lowest character." Even worse, Hamilton "practically deserted his wife for the lewd women who performed on his stage or gathered to witness the plays." The lascivious goings-on at the seedy establishment resulted in "numerous and emphatic" complaints, resulting in a police raid on the night of March 6, 1880. A group of detectives gathered at the rear of the building to block any escapees, while a van was driven to the front door, "and the police, entering suddenly, took possession of the stage and captured the actors."

In the humiliating trial that ensued, Mrs. Hamilton sat in court during her husband's proceedings, "acting the part of a faithful wife, notwithstanding his treachery to her." Friends and family were alarmed by the scandal's deleterious effects on Mrs. Hamilton's health and begged her to leave her disloyal husband. She refused. The ultimate blow came when, once again, Hamilton disappeared. His unwaveringly supportive wife heard nothing from him, "and her death from a broken heart [was] her reward for his fidelity." Hamilton, meanwhile, had long forgotten his devoted first wife and ended up in Illinois, where he married Mary Keogh, described in a local newspaper as a "beautiful belle of Bloomington, Ill."

Staying true to form, the restless Hamilton eventually deserted his new wife and infant son, heading south. He settled in Jackson, Mississippi, as a poultry farmer, married another woman and had another child. In 1915, he signed himself into a Civil War veterans' home in Dayton, Ohio, listing his occupation as "traveling salesman," and signed out a year later. Hamilton died on April 12, 1917. After a life of wild misadventure, public scandal and wild debauchery, the notorious rapscallion slipped quietly into obscurity. His final resting place is unknown.

ALEXANDER SPRINGSTEEN

Predecessor of Fame

He was, at one time, probably the most forgotten person of all the subjects of this book. In the modern era, however, his descendant, perhaps the most famous New Jerseyan in history, has been instrumental in the rediscovered story of Alexander Springsteen in their shared homeland, Monmouth County, New Jersey.

Born in 1822, Springsteen married Harriet Smith at Hedden's Corner in Monmouth County. The couple would have six children, four of whom survived to adulthood. In 1862, the forty-year-old farmer made what, in retrospect, seems a somewhat surprising decision considering his age: he joined the Union army.

In June 1862, President Abraham Lincoln asked the states for 300,000 three-year enlistment volunteer soldiers to expand the army, and New Jersey was requested to provide five regiments of approximately 1,000 men each. The units were, for the most part, regionally recruited, and Company A of the 14th New Jersey Volunteer Infantry, which Springsteen joined on August 11, 1862, as a private, was a Monmouth County unit. The 14th was organized at Camp Vredenburg, located at the Revolutionary War Monmouth Court House Battlefield west of Freehold, where Springsteen was formally mustered into service for three years' duty on August 26, 1862.

On the rainy morning of September 2, 1862, following a few barroom brawls in Freehold, the men of the 14th New Jersey packed their tents, boarded the cars of the Freehold and Jamesburg Agricultural Railroad and rolled off to war. Upon arrival in Baltimore, they did not, as most regiments did, go on to Washington, but rather took a train west, where the regiment was posted along the Monocacy River across from Frederick, Maryland, to guard a critical railway and river crossing. Some men were temporarily detached to escort Confederate prisoners from the Battle of Antietam to a POW camp.

The 14th remained at Monocacy for nine months, fortunately missing some of the bloodiest battles endured by the Army of the Potomac. While the regiment lost men to disease, there were no combat casualties. All in all, despite some problems with mud, it was a pleasant time for Private Springsteen and his fellow Jerseymen. The regiment's Major Peter Vredenburgh remarked that around the colonel's campfire "song and wit are there, flavored with the cracking of jokes and the cracking of hickory, making one feel as if he was enjoying a clam bake or evening frolic at home."

In the wake of Gettysburg, however, on July 9, 1863, the frolic ended, and things got far more serious. The 14th was ordered to join the Army of the Potomac and was assigned to the 1st Brigade of the 3rd Division of the III Army Corps. In November, on Thanksgiving Day, the 14th fought in its first battle, at Locust Grove, Virginia, and performed well but sustained a loss of sixteen men killed and fifty-eight wounded.

The 14th New Jersey spent the winter in a former Confederate camp and was transferred to the 1st Brigade of the 3rd Division of the VI Army Corps in the spring. The regiment was fully engaged in the Army of the Potomac's 1864 campaign, fighting at Wilderness, Spotsylvania, Cold Harbor and in the initial operations before Petersburg. As the bloody summer dragged on, Major Vredenburgh wrote home that "you can have no idea with what perfect indifference everyone seems to regard life out here." There were some high points. At Cold Harbor, Companies D and F and Springsteen's Company A broke through the enemy line and captured more than one hundred Confederate soldiers.

To relieve the pressure on his army, General Robert E. Lee ordered General Jubal Early's Corps to advance down the Shenandoah Valley to Maryland and threaten Washington in the summer of 1864. The VI Army Corps was sent to Maryland to protect the capital, with the 14th's brigade in the lead. Back on its old campground, the 14th and other units engaged the enemy along the Monocacy River. It was a bloody day. Major Vredenburgh was everywhere along the Union line, exhorting, cajoling and riding through a blizzard of bullets unscathed, seemingly living a charmed life. The 14th's color bearer, his flagstaff shattered by a bullet, went down with a fatal wound, and a man from Company F ran forward and shot down the

Alexander
Springsteen.
*Courtesy of the
Monmouth County
Historical Society.*

opposing Confederate color bearer. Eventually, the outnumbered Yankees withdrew, but they had accomplished their mission, delaying the Rebels until reinforcements reached Washington. The 14th lost ten men killed, sixty-nine wounded and five missing, but it saved the capital.

The regiment subsequently pursued Early's retreating army into the Shenandoah Valley as part of General Phil Sheridan's army, fighting in Union victories at Winchester, where Major Vredenburgh, in command of the regiment, was ordered to lead the 14th in an assault. He turned in his saddle and yelled above the din of musketry and artillery, "I'll do all I can for you boys." But he could do nothing for himself. A three-inch unexploded shell hit the major in his neck and pitched him off his horse. He was dead before he hit the ground. His regiment continued the assault, which was successful.

14th New Jersey Veterans dedicate their memorial at Monocacy battlefield. *Author's collection.*

Sheridan's army would fight Early's two more times, at Fisher's Hill and Cedar Creek, both Union victories. The VI Army Corps returned to Petersburg, where, on April 2, 1865, the regiment took part in the final breakthrough of the Confederate lines. There would be one more fight in the pursuit of Lee, at Sailors' Creek, the last engagement in which the 14th participated.

On June 8, the VI Corps was reviewed at Washington, and on June 19, the 14th New Jersey was formally mustered out, proceeding on the following day to Trenton, where, on June 19, the men "received their final pay, exchanged farewells and separated into the old familiar paths of peace, where from their feet had been lured only at the call of solemn and imperious duty." During the three years of its service, the 14th New Jersey lost 8 officers and 139 men killed or mortally wounded, as well as 110 men who died of disease.

Alexander Springsteen had, somewhat remarkably, survived his three years of war and returned to Monmouth County to work as a farm laborer and carpenter. He joined the local Grand Army of the Republic's Conover Post in Freehold and participated in the post's reunions and veterans' affairs.

In 1880, Springsteen applied for an army pension, stating that he was suffering from "lung and kidney" medical problems he had initially contracted in his service. He was awarded a pension and died on June 16, 1888, of "kidney disease." His obituary noted that he had been sick for the past year and had "recently suffered from paralysis." A delegation from the Conover GAR post attended his funeral. In July 1888, Harriet received a widow's pension.

Alexander Springsteen was "born in the USA," and he did his job for his country. His work ended human slavery and united his nation. He was not as famed as his talented great-great-grandson Bruce, but he paved the way.

GEORGE ASHBY

Sole Survivor

George Ashby was born in Burlington, New Jersey, on January 25, 1844. In 1864, Ashby, then living in Crosswicks, New Jersey, enlisted as a private in the 45th U.S. Colored Infantry, organized at Camp William Penn outside Philadelphia between June and August 1864. He was one of more than 2,900 African American Jerseymen who enlisted in the Union army. When the regiment arrived in Washington, D.C., four of its ten companies were detached for duty in defense of the capital, while the remaining companies, under the command of Colonel Ulysses Doubleday, continued south to City Point, Virginia, where they were assigned to the X Army Corps of the Army of the James, then engaged, along with the Army of the Potomac, along the Petersburg/Richmond line.

The 45th was engaged at New Market Heights, Fort Harrison and Darbytown Road. In December 1864, the unit was reunited with its four missing companies and transferred to the XXV Army Corps. The 45th took part in the final campaigns of the war in the East, through the surrender of the Army of Northern Virginia at Appomattox. The regiment was assigned to guard and occupation duty at Petersburg and City Point, Virginia, until May, when it was ordered, with the XXV Corps, to Texas on a dual mission. The French had invaded Mexico and installed a government in defiance of the Monroe Doctrine, and the force was intended to encourage them to leave, as well as to provide an occupying force in the former Confederate state.

45th USCT flag. *Courtesy of the New Jersey State Museum.*

Border duty was tough, due to the weather and an initial lack of logistical support. It was so hot that the overall commander of the expedition, General Phil Sheridan, was quoted as saying, "If I owned Texas and hell, I would rent out Texas and live in hell." Rations were, when available, limited to salt pork and hardtack. Scurvy ran rampant throughout the XXV Corps until supplies of fresh vegetables arrived in August.

On the plus side, one U.S. Colored Troop sergeant major reported, "If our regiment stays here any length of time, we will all speak Spanish, as we are learning very fast." The 45th was assigned to guard duty along the Mexican border in Brownsville until October, when the regiment returned to Philadelphia and was mustered out of service. During his time in the unit, Private Ashby had risen in rank to corporal and then sergeant and, finally, first sergeant of Company H. The latter rank not only required leadership skills but also the ability to read, write and keep records.

Sergeant Ashby was mustered out of the service at Philadelphia with the 45th in November 1865 and returned to his life as a New Jersey small farmer. In 1869, he married Phoebe Cole of Crosswicks and had nine children with her. He moved with his family to Allentown, New Jersey, and participated in the town's Fourth of July parades until 1942, when "the sole local survivor of the conflict between the Blues and the Grays" was

Sergeant George Ashby's grave. *Author's collection.*

relieved from that arduous duty and waved a flag from his porch as the parade passed by.

In January 1944, a reporter interviewed the old veteran, who was then celebrating his 100th birthday. Ashby predicted an Allied victory in World War II and stated that if he could, he would "enlist all over again." He took an active interest in the progress of the war and commented on various campaigns. The following year, when he was declared "Allentown's oldest resident," he was described as "still in fairly good health."

When George Ashby died at the age of 102 in Allentown on April 26, 1946, he was the last surviving New Jersey Civil War veteran. He had nine children, sixteen grandchildren, fourteen great-grandchildren and seven great-great-grandchildren at the time of his death. Ashby received a military funeral complete with color guard and firing squad provided by the Hamilton Township American Legion Post No. 31. He was buried at the Allentown African Methodist Episcopal Church Cemetery, now the Hamilton Street Cemetery. One of his grandchildren, Harold James Ashby, would go on to become deputy attorney general for the State of New Jersey. Sergeant Ashby's legacy lives on.

RODMAN McCAMLEY PRICE

A Governor Who Ended Up in Jail

R odman McCamley Price was born on May 5, 1816, in Newton, Sussex County, New Jersey, to an influential family. He attended the Presbyterian Academy at Lawrenceville and Princeton University before dropping out to study law under an attorney, and in 1840, he used political connections, as well as those of his wife, Matilda Tranchard, daughter of a naval officer, to become a navy purser, a position dealing with payroll and supply purchases. During the Mexican-American War, Price was appointed *alcalde* of Monterrey by Commodore John D. Sloat, making him the first American official to govern a municipality in California.

Price subsequently became purser for the Pacific Squadron, with headquarters in San Francisco, and engaged in land speculation and other businesses as a sideline to his official duties. A delegate to the California Constitutional Convention, he also ran unsuccessfully for Congress. Accused of misappropriating funds through unauthorized drafts of customhouse revenues and maintaining inadequate payroll records, Price was ordered east to give an account of his activities, but the charges were indefinitely postponed when the steamer carrying his records burned. He was sued by the U.S. Navy for $88,000 in missing funds, in a case that dragged on until resolved in his favor by a Senate bill exonerating him in 1890.

Out of the navy in 1850, Price moved to Hoboken and began speculating on Wall Street as well as in California real estate. Using his father's influence to gain the nomination, he was elected to one term in Congress from New Jersey's Fifth District as a Democrat. Failing reelection, he ran successfully for

Rodman McCamley Price.
Author's collection.

governor of the state in 1853, with "fiery apple brandy flowing freely at rallies." Governor Price reformed New Jersey's school system, opened the first "normal school" to train teachers, initiated the first geological survey of the state, collaborated with New York on harbor facility construction and expanded the state's judicial system and insane asylum.

Price had some grandiose ideas regarding his state and himself. He seemed to view New Jersey as his nation, dispatching Thomas Cadwallader, the state's militia adjutant general, to Europe to report back to him on small-arms innovations and manufacturing, although the federal government had already dispatched a highly regarded professional ordnance officer, Major Alfred Mordecai, on the same mission. Cadwallader did get to travel to England with former Paterson, New Jersey arms manufacturer Samuel Colt, and they apparently had an enjoyable time.

On the national level, Price was far less progressive than domestically. As a congressman, he had advocated flogging in the navy to maintain a "well ordered, well-disciplined ship" and supported expanding slavery into the territories. To Price, slavery was "no sin," but rather a normal way of conducting race relations.

After his term as governor, Price opened a ferry service from Weehawken to New York City. He campaigned for Stephen A. Douglas in 1860 and in February 1861 was a delegate to the "Peace Conference" convened in Washington to head off the Civil War. Once war broke out, however, he advocated that New Jersey remain neutral or even join the Confederacy, effectively ending his political career. When abolition became a war aim in 1863, Price ranted that Lincoln was "a traitor" who "stands reeking in the blood of his countrymen." Ironically, Price's son Francis, commissioned a first lieutenant in the 7th New Jersey Infantry in 1861, eventually rose to the rank of brevet brigadier general in the Union army.

In the postwar era, Rodman Price moved from Weehawken to the Ramapo Valley, where he bought a farm near Oakland, New Jersey, and engaged in numerous failing business activities. In the early 1890s, revived inquiries into an alleged 1850 real estate swindle in California resulted in his imprisonment. He was released due to ill health, died on June 7, 1894, in Oakland and was buried in nearby Mahwah.

ROBERT HARRIOT

"Mickey Free"

By the middle of the nineteenth century, spectator sports had evolved beyond watching daredevils jumping to their potential doom, and the most popular event was watching people participate in walking competitions.

Robert Harriot was born in Ireland in 1819 and began a "race performance" career at the age of fifteen. Harriot gained a reputation competing throughout the British Isles in walking and running competitions, which often featured additional tasks like picking up stones, vaulting hurdles or walking a thin wooden plank. Monetary prizes were awarded, and spectators gambled on the outcomes of these contests. Harriot immigrated to Jersey City in 1850 and continued as a professional "pedestrian," famed for walking "a thousand miles in a thousand hours." His carefree persona earned him the nickname "Mickey Free" after a character in the popular novel *Charles O'Malley: The Irish Dragoon*. In May 1852, Harriot married Eliza Fox in Newark. The couple had eight children. Eliza took up her husband's trade and became well known as a female competitor in the 1850s. "Mickey Free and Mrs. Free" were the only known performing "pedestrian couple."

In February 1861, when President-elect Lincoln visited Jersey City, Harriot, dressed as a "Wide Awake," a Republican activist, climbed the speakers' dais, shook Lincoln's hand, patted him on the back and was promptly clubbed off the platform by a policeman, much to the crowd's amusement. In August 1861, he enlisted in Company C of the 5th New Jersey Infantry, where his celebrity presence was noted by diarist Alfred Bellard. At the Battle of Williamsburg in May 1862, Harriot lost several fingers to a

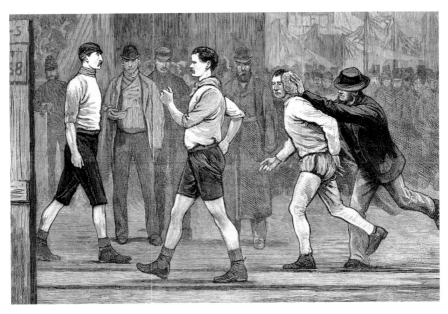

Nineteenth-century pedestrian competition. The man on the right is getting his sweat wiped off. *Author's collection.*

shell fragment, and during his convalescence in a Philadelphia hospital, he walked home to Jersey City for a visit.

Harriot was discharged for disability in February 1863, awarded a pension in April and reenlisted as a private in Company B, 33rd New Jersey Infantry in August. Most of his service in the 33rd was as a hospital orderly, and he was mustered out in July 1865. A civilian again, Harriot returned to New Jersey to continue his career, albeit briefly and with limited success, as age and military service took a toll on his body. He became a mason and stonecutter and later Jersey City dog pound master, and he built a "home on wheels," which he relocated around the city periodically.

Always a colorful character, Harriot had several run-ins with the law, including charges of shooting at his wife and perjury. Robert "Mickey Free" Harriot died on November 21, 1878, of pneumonia and is buried at Holy Name Cemetery, Jersey City.

CHARLES HOPKINS

New Jersey Civil War Hero

Here's the story of a genuine New Jersey hero: Charles Hopkins, born on May 16, 1842, in Hope, New Jersey. He worked with his father, an Underground Railroad conductor, in helping escaped slaves make their way to freedom.

A man willing to stand up and fight for his beliefs, Hopkins joined the 1st New Jersey Infantry as a private after the outbreak of the Civil War. At the Battle of Gaines's Mill, Virginia, on June 27, 1862, although wounded several times himself, he carried his badly wounded sergeant, Richard Donnelly, off the field under heavy fire. Hopkins was awarded the Medal of Honor for his selfless bravery.

Promoted to corporal, Hopkins was captured at the Battle of the Wilderness in May 1864 and spent most of the rest of the war in the infamous Andersonville prisoner of war stockade. Hopkins kept the names of his fellow Jerseymen who died at Andersonville as well as the locations of their burials in a diary. He was a prime mover in establishing the New Jersey monument in the cemetery there in 1898. After the war, he served as mayor of Boonton, a county freeholder and in various other positions, including as a member of the New Jersey State Assembly and an officer in the Army and Navy Legion of Valor.

In the 1890s, former sergeant Donnelly, then the New Jersey National Guard's quartermaster general, spoke with Hopkins, discovered that he had never received his awards (even though they had been authorized in 1862) and contacted the War Department on his behalf. The old soldier finally

New Jersey Monument at Andersonville. *Courtesy of the National Park Service.*

Hopkins, his wife and his belated medal. *Author's collection.*

received his medal and certificate. The photo with this essay, of Hopkins and his wife, Hettie, mother of his seven children, dates from 1927. The medal around Hopkins's neck in the photo is not the Civil War version of the award. When Charles Hopkins died on February 14, 1934, he was the last surviving New Jersey Civil War Medal of Honor recipient.

In 2012, one of Hopkins's descendants, Charles Maraziti, gave an audiovisual presentation on Hopkins at the Montville Township Historical Society. Included in the presentation was a display of Hopkins's "Medal of Honor Certificate, his ceremonial sword and an invitation from President Woodrow Wilson to the General Phil Kearny equestrian statue unveiling."

CLARENCE HETRICK

Asbury Park's Notable Mayor

Clarence Hetrick's beginnings were unassuming enough. He was born and raised in the sleepy town of Van Wert, Ohio, earning the unflattering nickname of "Toad" as he grew into adolescence. Even during those early years, however, Hetrick embodied a precocity and ambition that would eventually elevate him to the highest levels of Monmouth County, New Jersey politics, where he would experience the best and worst of life in that rarefied circle of local movers and shakers.

Hetrick began his climb into the world of local power and privilege soon after the family moved east to Monmouth County, New Jersey, in 1887. He was the first student from the county to win an academic scholarship to Rutgers University, graduating in 1895. Initially employed at his father's real estate firm, Hetrick took over the family business following the elder Hetrick's death in 1899. In 1906, he solidified his position in the community by marrying Ida Wyckoff, a member of an old New Jersey and Monmouth County family.

Immersing himself in local Republican politics, Hetrick worked his way through a series of high-profile municipal jobs, including one as Asbury Park treasurer following the city's 1906 absorption of the West Park section of town, where he lived. Capitalizing on his growing political experience and popularity, Hetrick secured the position of Monmouth County sheriff in 1907, despite rumors that he had a mistress who was a laundress at a local laundry. For young Hetrick, life was good, but looming ahead was a community tragedy that would threaten his career and test his personal and moral courage.

The crisis began when ten-year-old Marie Smith, a white girl, went missing near Asbury and Ridge Avenues on her way home from school in November 1910. A massive search involving police, schoolboys and National Guardsmen was launched, and rumors flew, including one that suggested the girl might have been abducted by Romani then camping in nearby Ardena. When her battered body was discovered several days later, Trent Williams, a Black handyman who worked for the girl's aunt, with whom Marie and her parents lived, was arrested on suspicion of being her murderer.

Williams, also known as "Black Diamond," strongly protested his innocence but was incarcerated at the Asbury Park jail. Shortly afterward, a mob began to form, and there was considerable talk of a vigilante solution to the crime. Sheriff Hetrick and Asbury Park police chief William H. Smith were understandably nervous and bolstered security. Hetrick himself holstered a handgun to help protect the prisoner, and then, "thwarting a surging mob of would-be lynchers armed with sledgehammers, axes, crowbars and other jail-breaking implements," they secretly transferred Williams to Freehold for safekeeping.

Frank Heidemann, a German immigrant who worked for an Asbury Park florist, was also considered an initial suspect in the Smith murder, since he had been spotted peeking over a fence at the girl while she was playing. Heidemann was arrested shortly after Williams but released three weeks later for lack of evidence. On December 2, a Monmouth County grand jury found that Marie "had met her death at the hands of some person unknown to this jury" via a blunt instrument. The jury could not conclude whether the girl had been sexually molested.

Despite the conflict, the still-incarcerated Williams remained the prime suspect. Black Diamond's case was not helped when Martha Coleman, a local young woman, testified that she heard Williams say that "there was a little white girl at Mrs. Jackson's [Marie's aunt] whom he intended to possess."

Hetrick remained unconvinced of Williams's guilt. The sheriff thought that Heidemann, who left town shortly after his release, was the real murderer. Along with some respected citizens who agreed with his conclusion, the sheriff hired the Burns Detective Agency to investigate the case, much to the dismay of the local police.

Hetrick's judgment eventually proved correct. In March 1911, an undercover Burns private detective who had befriended the unsuspecting German and traveled around the country with him "wormed" a confession out of the gardener. The citizens of Asbury Park were "greatly stirred up" by the arrest and subsequent trial, conviction and execution. Sheriff Hetrick's efforts in clearing Thomas Williams were not forgotten by Asbury's West Side African American community, which delivered landslide votes for him when he ran for Asbury Park city commissioner in 1915 and was subsequently elected mayor by his four fellow commissioners.

The following years were halcyon ones for Hetrick, who proved to be an energetic city leader. Life at the top of the local political heap, however, left Hetrick vulnerable to attack, and his name was temporarily tarnished by a Roaring Twenties scandal that centered on a raucous speakeasy party.

Hetrick was not only mayor of Asbury Park but also president of the city's chamber of commerce and the biggest booster of Asbury's transformation into a modern resort and local economic center. It was his involvement with the Asbury Park business community that provided an opportunity for the Ku Klux Klan, a white supremacist group enjoying a resurgence among those who felt threatened by the country's breathless pace of societal change, to spring a trap. The Klan, allied with Asbury Park's

Clarence Hetrick. *Author's collection.*

conservative anti-Hetrick old guard, attempted a coup that would remove him from office on charges of immoral activity.

In the spring of 1924, Hetrick attended the city's annual trade fair, followed by a dinner and cabaret entertainment at the Deal Inn with leading Asbury Park and Monmouth County merchants and political leaders. Following the event, Walter Tindall, an Asbury Park printer who attended, claimed it had turned into an orgy in which he had refused to participate. Tindall was a covert Klansman, and his statement instantly galvanized the Civic Church League and the Klan against the mayor. According to Tindall's affidavit, there was "much drinking" at the affair, and "five women from New York gave an improper display."

Hetrick vigorously denied the accusations. The mayor firmly stated that "any allegation to the effect that nude women were present is a lie pure and simple" and emphatically declared that "the charge that a nude woman sat on my lap is a damnable lie." The charges collapsed when no one corroborated Tindall's accusations, and he was revealed as an apparent bankrupt Klan puppet beholden to local Klan leaders. Tindall's account was summarily dismissed by a county grand jury, and he was charged with perjury. The mayor's triumph broke the back of the Klan in Asbury Park.

In the years that followed, Hetrick continued to serve as mayor, playing a major role in local politics. Somewhere along the way, however, the financial whiz-kid and community advocate began to evolve into someone capable of questionable and unsavory actions. Hetrick as political reformer began to morph into Hetrick the political boss. He splurged on Asbury improvement projects during the frenetic 1920s but failed to heed the onset of the ever-deepening Great Depression. Although Asbury Park was hard hit by the economic collapse, Hetrick and his cronies continued to indulge themselves.

Hetrick's expanding boardwalk construction program increased the city debt to $15 million by 1930, and boardwalk lease fees to his friends were lower than ever. Probable kickbacks on those leases were only one source of dubious money that Mayor Hetrick was raking in. Abetted by city administrators, Hetrick became increasingly involved in shady local affairs. Imported voters allegedly participated in city elections for "four bits and a shot of rum." Mobsters and bootleggers acquired permits to carry concealed handguns from the Asbury Park Police Department based on phony local hotel addresses. The beachfront that Hetrick rebuilt at city expense not only failed to turn a profit but also suffered increasingly deep deficits.

In 1933, outraged citizens formed a reform ticket to unseat Hetrick and succeeded. He returned to power in a 1935 recall election, and despite his promise to solve the city's "acute problems," he quickly returned to his old ways of corrupt cronyism. Within months of his return, Hetrick and his councilmen narrowly escaped jail on a contempt of court charge resulting from a lawsuit filed by unpaid city bondholders. By the spring of 1941, a new reform ticket managed to defeat Hetrick, despite his promise of immense progress and trickle-down prosperity.

Soon after, Hetrick died of diabetes and thrombosis, ending a once-stellar career on a sour note of defeat and dissolution. The once-admired Hetrick had succumbed to the temptations of power and influence, and his final years were a bitter reflection of his failings.

PETER J. McGUIRE

The Father of Labor Day

Peter J. McGuire was born the son of Irish immigrants in New York City on July 6, 1852. A bright young man, McGuire got a job in a dry goods store at the age of eleven, attended the Cooper Institute at night and was involved in labor organizing early on. Described as "an itinerant cabinet maker," he moved to St. Louis, where he became a woodworker in a piano factory, joined the Knights of Labor, led a strike and, reportedly, came up with the idea for a holiday called "Labor Day."

Instrumental in the founding of the Carpenters and Joiners Union, as well as the American Federation of Labor (AFL), McGuire was a friend of the first AFL president, Samuel Gompers. He was also involved in politics as a member of the Greenback Labor Party. Demonized as a "radical" and a "fanatic," McGuire was jailed during a labor dispute in Cleveland, Ohio. Despite his fiery reputation, however, the idea of a holiday to honor labor gained mainstream attention, and New York City held its first "Labor Day" parade in 1882.

In the 1880s, McGuire moved back east to Camden, New Jersey, where he spent the rest of his life. In 1887, the legislatures of New Jersey, New York, Oregon and Massachusetts declared Labor Day an official state holiday, and Congress made it a national holiday in 1894.

McGuire, as with many charismatic organization leaders, developed enemies within and without the labor movement. Although he had spent much of his own money on Carpenters and Joiners Union affairs, he was accused of embezzlement and voted out as the union's leader in 1902.

Left: Peter McGuire. *Author's collection.*

Below: McGuire Memorial. *Author's collection.*

McGuire died in Camden, apparently due to excessive alcohol consumption, on February 18, 1906. A newspaper reported that he had "died with two cents in his pockets."

Peter J. McGuire was buried at Arlington Cemetery in Pennsauken, New Jersey, and a 1937 newspaper article described his final resting place as "ever a shrine at which the loyal labor unionist bows on Memorial Day." As the years went by, a visit to his grave by labor leaders, as well as politicians interested in currying favor with labor unions, became an annual ritual.

In 1952, internal disputes long forgotten, the International Brotherhood of Carpenters and Joiners subscribed $100,000 to establish a memorial to McGuire featuring a marble statue of the "father of Labor Day" at his grave site. The accompanying photo shows union officials M.A. Hutcheson (*left*) and O.W. Blaier at the dedication in August 1952. McGuire was inducted into the New Jersey Hall of Fame in 2014.

Interestingly, a recently discovered 1894 article published in the *Paterson Evening Call* credited Paterson alderman and labor leader Matthew Maguire as the "undisputed author of Labor Day as a Holiday." It seems more than likely, however, that the credit belongs to Peter.

WILLIAM REDDAN

World War I Hero

William Reddan was born in England in 1883 to Irish parents. He immigrated to the United States with his mother and sister in 1895 and lived in New York City before moving to New Jersey. In 1904, he joined the New Jersey National Guard as a private and became a naturalized American citizen in 1906. Reddan rose through the ranks to become a captain by 1914.

In June 1916, Reddan's Company H of the 5th New Jersey Infantry Regiment, based in Orange, New Jersey, was mobilized, along with other New Jersey National Guard units, for duty in Douglas, Arizona, on the Mexican border in response to Mexican revolutionary Pancho Villa's incursion into New Mexico. While the regular army pursued Villa's forces into Mexico, the Jerseymen and other National Guardsmen deployed to the border did not engage in combat and suffered no casualties during their tour of duty, as there was a legal impediment to using them on foreign soil, but they did participate in some long, grueling marches.

The men of the 5th Regiment returned home in November but were activated again on March 25, 1917, as war with Germany became imminent, and deployed to guard bridges, railroads and other critical sites in the state until transferred to Camp McClellan, Alabama, in early September, where Company H was consolidated with Montclair's Company K of the 5th to create Company B of the 114th Infantry Regiment in the 29th Division.

Reddan was in command of Company B on October 12, 1918, when the unit was ordered to make a suicidal frontal assault on a German position at Bois D'Ormont, France, in the most savage battle New Jersey soldiers had been involved in since the 1st New Jersey Brigade stormed the Confederate line at Spotsylvania in 1864. Reddan was wounded but survived. Only thirteen men out of his company came out of the fight unscathed. The experience scarred him forever, and in 1936, he wrote and self-published a book titled *Other Men's Lives*, in which he described his service in the war and the battle. He assigned blame for his company's horrendous casualties on the higher American command, which he believed was oblivious to the strength of the German position, something the French unit on his flank had realized and halted. After the battle, a French officer, while praising the Jerseymen's courage,

Captain William Reddan.
Courtesy of the Reddan family.

pointed to his head and commented that they also must be "*beaucoup de malade ici*" (very crazy in the head).

Reddan's book told the story thus: "The first sergeant reported the company assembled. I looked them over and counted thirteen men. Were my eyes deceiving me? Thirteen men and myself? All that was left of 153 men and five officers who had gone into action twelve hours earlier.…To explain my feelings at the moment is impossible. I have never felt more alone at any time in my life."

Reddan was in Paris when the Armistice ending hostilities went into effect on November 11, 1918, and he remembered, "It is hard to imagine which place I would rather have been in when the order to 'cease firing' was given, on the front lines or in Paris; neither place will ever be forgotten. All in the A.E.F. [American Expeditionary Forces] were mighty proud of the fact that we had played a small part in helping to bring the war to an end. But especially proud of being soldiers or sailors of the United States." He concluded, "To all who served in Company B, 114th US Infantry, the 'Skipper' salutes you. Au revoir, mes braves."

Reddan rejoined the National Guard after the war and was awarded the New Jersey Distinguished Service Medal "for bravery in France" by Governor A. Harry Moore at the National Guard Training Center in Sea Girt in 1927. In 1933, then Major Reddan was "decorated with the silver star" by Governor Moore to accompany his Purple Heart, retiring as a major.

Reddan was active in veterans affairs in the postwar years, was organizer and first commander of American Legion Post 190 in Orange, New Jersey, and became the town's police court clerk and tax assessor. Three of Reddan's four sons served in World War II. The one who did not was still in high school. Reddan once said that should his book ever be made into a film, he would like Gary Cooper to play him. Looking at his photo, we can see why.

William Reddan resided at 196 Inwood Avenue in Montclair, New Jersey, and vacationed at his summer home in Manasquan, where, while fishing on the beach on July 1, 1944, Major Reddan, one of New Jersey's unsung war heroes who had never quite recovered from being wounded and gassed in World War I, suffered a fatal heart attack at the age of sixty-one. He was buried at Immaculate Conception Cemetery in Montclair. Reddan's book was recently reprinted in soft cover format by Westholme Publishing.

MILDRED E. GILLARS

Axis Sally in Camden

This book tells the tales of forgotten New Jerseyans who were either born and raised in or moved to the state and spent a significant portion of their lives there, gaining fame in their day for distinguished behavior or extreme rascality. Mildred E. Gillars was an exception, at least in residence. She spent but a few weeks in New Jersey in 1928, during which time, using the name "Mrs. Barbara Elliot," she walked into the office of the Camden, New Jersey *Courier Post*, known for its affinity for sensational stories, and announced emotionally that her "runaway husband Charles Elliot," last seen in Camden, had abandoned her and the infant in her womb.

Gillars/Elliot stayed at the Hotel Walt Whitman, and the next morning she called the desk clerk and asked him to go to her room. He did and found a complex suicide note, which made the front page of the *Courier Post* and spread from there to New York papers and wire services. The Camden police were advised, and although some were aware of the possibility that this was all a publicity stunt, they decided to err on the side of caution. On the misty morning of October 19, 1928, Camden police officer William Basier was patrolling the bridge to Philadelphia when he saw a female figure take off her coat and dangle a foot off the bridge. He reacted and raced toward her, grabbing her as she leaned toward the water, 135 feet below. She protested, but he escorted her to police headquarters, where a bevy of journalists and photographers had gathered to see Mrs. Elliot. In police court, she maintained her right to commit suicide. That story made the front page as well, and she was kept in protective custody for the weekend.

Mildred Gillars in Camden Police Court, 1928. *Author's collection.*

Her "husband," a New York writer whose real name was John Ramsey, showed up at the *Courier Post* the following day, claiming that he was Charles Elliot, and was escorted to the police station, where "Barbara" dramatically staged a fainting spell on his arrival. Presented with accumulated evidence throwing doubt on their story, Ramsey quickly confessed that he and Gillars had been offered seventy-five dollars each by a public relations firm to stage an event to publicize a movie titled *Unwanted Children*. Gillars then "confessed that her leaping and loving and sobbing and fainting were a hoax."

In police court, Gillars apologized for her hoax. She and her pretend husband were sentenced to three months in jail, but the sentence was suspended if they left town immediately. Unfortunately, the motion picture publicity firm hadn't forwarded their salaries, and Gillars and Ramsey were broke. Local newspaper boys, whose sales had peaked because of the story, took pity, however, and "chipped in" to help the duo get home. One lad told them, "You did your best to put it over," adding that the show "was worth carfare back to New York," which was $12.75.

"Putting it over" became Mildred "Midge" Gillars's life story. She was born in Portland, Maine, in 1900 as Mildred Sisk. Her father was a drunk

64

and was divorced by her mother, Mae, who remarried a dentist, Robert Gillars, who was also an alcoholic and, some say, incestuous. The family moved from state to state, ending up in Ohio. Gillars attended Ohio Wesleyan University, where she studied acting and drama for four years and "had a flair for drama," but she failed to graduate. She then headed for New York, with a show business career in mind. The career failed to materialize, and the Camden incident was a highlight. In 1931, she followed her then lover to Algeria.

In 1934, Gillars left North Africa and met up with her mother, who was on a European tour in Budapest, and they traveled to Germany. Mae returned to America, but her daughter elected to stay in Adolf Hitler's Third Reich, where she took a job teaching English and wrote a few articles and reviews, in which her biographer detected a hint of anti-Semitism.

By 1940, "Midge" was broke again and took a job at the German state radio. The United States was not yet involved in World War II, and short-wave radio broadcasts to the country emphasized that neutrality was the best course for the nation to follow, praising the "America First" movement. The Germans did have a problem, though, with their announcers delivering fake news about the impending British collapse speaking in German accents. The answer was Gillars, with her midwestern American accent and soothing voice, who was able to turn a rant against Franklin Roosevelt, Jewish people and the British, accompanied by popular swing music, into a pleasant advisory on "truth."

Gillars apparently thought that the United States would not enter the war, as she was frozen in the 1920s view that World War I was a mistake and that the country would not enter another conflict to expand the British and French colonial empires. She was also engaged to a German citizen, who was later killed on the Eastern Front in the Soviet Union. She then became the mistress of Max Otto Koischwitz, a married former Hunter College professor who had returned to Germany from New York before the war and oversaw Nazi radio broadcasts to American troops once the United States entered the conflict. By 1943, she was reportedly the highest-paid performer on German radio.

Under Koischwitz, Gillars expanded her repertoire to star in radio plays and conduct interviews with American POWs. As it turned out, American soldiers chuckled at her propaganda broadcasts and loved her swing music. She gained the GI nickname "Axis Sally" and would often suggest to her listeners, "I just wonder if your girl isn't sort of running around with 4Fs," which no doubt reminded GIs of their humorous drill song "Am I Right or Wrong?," with the line "Ain't no use in goin' home/Jody's got your girl and gone."

Her mentor's wife was killed in a bombing raid in 1943, and while Gillars was sure that he would then marry her, he died unexpectedly in 1944. As the war ended, she tried to fade away into the droves of refugees swarming across Europe but was nabbed by U.S. Army counterintelligence agents in Berlin in 1946 and returned to the United States, where she was charged with treason. Ironically, had she married Koischwitz, who was a German citizen, and thus likely became a citizen of the Reich herself, she might not have been charged with treason.

Gillars was charged with ten counts of treason, later reduced to eight, and went on trial in 1949. She had tried to evade outright treasonous statements during her broadcasts and claimed that she did the shows out of love for Koischwitz. Reporters noted her "flamboyance and cool self-possession" and that she "cut a theatrical figure in tight fitting black dresses" in the courtroom. Those attributes might have helped her out with the jury, which only convicted her on one count, for a play in which she portrayed a woman who dreamed that her son was killed in an invasion of Europe. She was fined $10,000 and sentenced to ten to thirty years in prison.

Gillars was released on parole in 1961 and, having converted to Catholicism while in prison, was granted refuge in a Columbus, Ohio convent of the Sisters of the Poor Child Jesus, where she taught music and tutored students. She returned to Ohio Wesleyan, got her degree and lived quietly until she passed away of colon cancer at the age of eighty-seven in 1988.

The Camden fiasco was literally the opening act in a rather bizarre career, and like many, it began in New Jersey. Many years later, a newspaper referred to Gillars's having had a "soap opera life." It was an accurate characterization. For the complete details of Mildred Gillars's life, see Richard Lucas's biography, *Axis Sally: The American Voice of Nazi Germany*.

ELLIS PARKER

The Rise and Fall of New Jersey's
Sherlock Holmes

Ellis Parker, the nationally known Burlington County detective chief who was instrumental in solving many of his county and New Jersey's crimes of his era, became interested in the Lindbergh baby kidnapping in 1932. His initial investigative contact was Paul Wendel, a pharmacist and attorney he had known for some time. Wendel had argued a case before the New Jersey Court of Chancery in 1919 and had forged documents to support his client. His deception was uncovered, and he was tried and convicted of perjury, sentenced to nine months in the Mercer County Workhouse and lost his law license as a result. In 1924, Wendel, who was then working as a real estate agent, received a pardon, based on letters of support from, among others, Ellis Parker, who knew his father, a prominent minister. Wendel received his law license back the following year, and the two developed a friendship of sorts.

In the immediate aftermath of the Lindbergh kidnapping, Wendel contacted Parker, suggesting that he could help with the investigation and indicating that he had contacts with criminal elements in Chicago and New York who might provide information on the location of the child and perhaps arrange his return. Parker, who was apparently miffed that he had not been assigned to find the kidnappers and had a longstanding feud with New Jersey State Police superintendent Herbert Norman Schwarzkopf, accepted the offer, no doubt hoping that he could uncover evidence of state police incompetence in the investigation.

Ellis Parker. *Author's collection.*

However, after allegedly following a series of improbable leads, including the possible involvement of Al Capone in the crime, Wendel turned up nothing, but he appears to have conned Parker, "America's Sherlock Holmes," out of some expense money.

As time went by and the Lindbergh baby's body was discovered, Wendell assured Parker that the corpse was not that of the Lindbergh child, and Parker began to think that perhaps Wendel had somehow been involved in the crime himself. He recalled that Wendel, a narcissist whose sense of grandiosity was apparent to anyone who knew him, had once declared that if he had $50,000, he would become great—and the ransom demanded was $50,000.

The arrest, trial and conviction of Bruno Richard Hauptmann in the case did not dissuade Parker from his opinion that others were involved, including possibly Wendel. This, along with his innate desire to show up the state police, led him to eagerly accept a request to reinvestigate the case from Governor Harold Hoffman, who had visited Hauptmann in his death row cell and was not convinced of his guilt either. Hoffman gave Hauptmann a thirty-day reprieve while Parker worked on the case.

Following Hoffman's request, Parker, with his son Ellis Jr. in charge of the actual operations, hired some dubious characters to kidnap Wendel, who was then living in New York to avoid prosecution on several New Jersey bad check charges. Parker's men forced Wendel into a car on February 14, 1936, and took him to a house in Brooklyn, where they confined him in a cellar, knocked him around and demanded he confess that he had kidnapped the Lindbergh baby. Ellis Parker Jr. apparently appeared and told Wendel that he would return him to New Jersey if he signed a confession, which he did.

Once back in Trenton, via Mount Holly, Wendel denied a connection to the kidnapping and said that his confession was forced through "torture." He displayed bruises from the beatings he had received, and it was apparent that he had no real connection with any of the physical evidence in the case. A grand jury refused to consider the charges, and Attorney General David Wilentz, who had personally prosecuted Hauptmann, referred to the Wendel affair as "the most vile fraud ever perpetrated on New Jersey."

Ironically, although Governor Hoffman refused to extradite the Parkers to New York to face trial in the Wendel affair, federal kidnapping charges were brought against the detective and his son under the new Lindbergh Law. They were convicted. Ellis Parker was sentenced to six years in Lewisburg prison and died there after six months, and his son served three years.

Ellis Parker Jr. was pardoned by President Harry Truman in 1947. Paul Wendel went on to a long career in the field of alternative medicine. He became an associate of Dr. Benedict Lust, a German-born founder of the American Naturopathy Society. In 1944, Wendel claimed that he was a "Doctor of Metaphysics" but was arrested in Kings County, New York, in 1946 and spent six months in jail for practicing medicine without a license. He self-published several books on various dubious medical procedures and gained some of the fame he so desperately wanted from adherents of the fringe medical community before dying in 1956.

WILLIAM GILBERT

Trenton's Freelance Executioner

W hen you are tired of your job, become an entrepreneur. In November 1922, William S. Gilbert of Trenton, New Jersey, got bored with his job as a night watchman at a rubber mill and did just that. He decided to take up another, more exciting and lucrative career, "making some easy money." He had some cards printed up that read "William S. Gilbert, Contracting Executioner," and sent them to the wardens of state prisons around the country, "asking that he be given the job of performing the execution of murderers sentenced to die." He told an inquiring reporter that he had been "commissioned to 'do his stuff' at a western prison some time in February."

Gilbert kept track of newspaper accounts of death sentences. In December 1922, an Illinois newspaper reported that he had advised a judge that he was willing to go to that state and perform an impending execution for a fee and travel expenses and "gave the warden of the New Jersey penitentiary as a reference to his ability and dexterity with the noose." Gilbert's efforts were apparently successful, as the "itinerant executioner," whose home base remained in Trenton, was the subject of a profile in a Wisconsin newspaper in December 1926.

Gilbert told the Wisconsin reporter an apocryphal tale of how he got his start in the business, saying that he had been a prison inmate and the warden, reluctant to execute a prisoner, told him that if he would do the job he would be released immediately. According to Gilbert, "that poor fellow asked me to pray for him before I sprung the trap. I got as far as 'Thy Kingdom Come' and then dropped him through. They criticized me for not finishing the prayer, but being my first job, I was nervous."

William Gilbert. *Author's collection.*

By 1926, Gilbert had executed forty men across the country. He told an inquiring reporter, "I'm proud of my record. And I stand ready to snuff 'em out just as fast as the court convicts 'em." A perpetual publicity seeker, he added that executions should return to being public spectacles as a deterrent to potential murderers, saying, "Many men, if they ever witnessed a hanging, would hesitate longer before killing another." At the time, he was distributing souvenir knives inscribed "William S. Gilbert, contracting executioner, Trenton, N.J. That's my business. I execute the death penalty in all its forms."

Gilbert was described in a Lincoln, Nebraska newspaper in October 1928 as "the man who sends men to their everlasting without blinking an eye." The paper noted that he was on his way from Trenton to execute Frank Sharp, convicted on circumstantial evidence of killing his wife. Gilbert had apparently expanded his skill set, keeping up with the times, as he was going to pull the switch when Sharp was scheduled to "take the [electric] chair."

In 1929, an Ohio newspaper characterized Gilbert as "a contracting headsman" who was "finishing his 58th job." By that time, he had executed fifty-six men and two women. When he told a reporter that "my latest job was my hardest," he was referring to his electrocution of Sharp.

Gilbert quickly acquired expertise in electrocution as well as hanging. On one case in Nebraska, he had to deliver two massive doses of electricity to convicted triple murderer Henry Sherman, commenting afterward that the twenty-two-year-old man was "a tough baby. I hate to give this second jolt."

Stories on Gilbert and his unique entrepreneurial occupation disappeared from the press after 1929. He may have taken on a more mundane but secure job. The 1930 census lists a William S. Gilbert living at 176 Ferry Street in Trenton and working as a city policeman.

ALMA WHITE

Queen of the KKK

It was a packed house at the tenth and final day of the annual Pillar of Fire camp meeting at the religious enclave of Zarephath, New Jersey. On that August night in 1933, devotees filled the tabernacle, a large, austere hall filled with movie theater–style seats.

A large part of the service consisted of testimonies by various members of the congregation. A local newspaper noted, "Some of them roll glibly from tongues that have evidently uttered them before, while others come haltingly and nervously. Some have a dramatic note and others sound simple and sincere."

Then, as "fever ran high," various men rose from their seats and to the music of "Onward, Christian Soldiers" walked round and round in front of the pulpit. After marching up and down the aisles, the men returned to their seats, where "they began gleeful little leaps into the air which ended in bounding jumps not unlike the old Charlston [*sic*]."

During this demonstration, Bishop Alma White—the star attraction— entered the church and quietly took her place on the platform. A reporter described her as "a large, bulky woman whose looks belie her true age of 71 years." As she rose to speak, an air of expectation filled the crowded hall.

What was expected to be a formal, prepared speech instead turned into a fiery warning of "just what happens to those who do not become converted before death," a reporter wrote. "An old-fashioned description of the hereafter almost reeked of hellfire and brimstone."

Such was the world of Bishop Alma White, a determined woman who rose from an impoverished childhood on a small farm in the hills of Kentucky to become the founder of the Pillar of Fire Church and its vast network of schools, colleges and radio stations.

Although one observer hailed White and her followers as "an independent, congenial group who manage very nicely," there was a darker side to White and the organization. White was a fierce feminist, but only in the service of white Protestant women. She was strongly anti-Catholic, anti-Semitic and anti-immigrant and became a prominent Ku Klux Klan supporter. White believed the Klan would help her attain her goal of liberating white Protestant

Alma White. *Author's collection.*

womanhood while keeping minorities and people of other religions "in their place." A dark undercurrent of intolerance ran beneath the self-righteous surface of White's religious doctrine.

White's early years were marked by poverty and a lack of opportunity. "Perhaps no person in the public eye today had come up through harder knocks to the stage of success in life than Alma White," noted a 1946 newspaper article. She was born in 1862 to a family of eleven children, and "she knew what it was to struggle for an existence."

Although her parents, William and Mary Bridwell, were determined to provide their children with an education, "it was Alma White's ill-fortune to be considered the dullest one of the family." She was kept at home much of the time to help with house and farm work.

Young Alma yearned to attend school, and she was finally allowed to attend for a short time. Much to her family's surprise, the bashful girl was an excellent student and eventually earned her teaching certificate. At the age of nineteen, she was chosen to stay with an aunt in the wilds of Montana, where she began teaching missionary work.

In 1887, Alma married Kent White, a ministerial student. As a minister's wife, she took an active interest in pastoral work, although her church gave no official recognition to women's ministry. Alma White devoted considerable time to missionary work and occasionally spoke from her husband's pulpit.

The Whites established a church in Denver, but Alma apparently separated from Kent and became estranged from Methodism as well. In 1907, she moved to New Jersey, where she founded the Pillar of Fire Church on a donated farm in the Somerset County community of Zarephath. White was ordained a bishop of her own church by a traveling Methodist evangelist. She then established her own Bible school, Zarephath Academy, on the farm. Zarephath dispatched evangelist recruiters across the country.

White's religious community was labeled by a Red Bank, New Jersey newspaper as "an experiment in communism as well as religion" following revival services held at Port Monmouth in 1921. Another news account noted that White's followers "gave themselves unrestrainedly to the singing of hymns, particularly the more rousing ones, and their services were spiced by the playing of marches. To these, the audience was free to clap its hands and wave its arms, but any further manifestation of religious fervor was frowned upon by the founder."

Some of her followers had once tried tricks of fainting and ecstasy, White recalled in a 1937 interview, but it didn't last for long. The stern minister told them, "You get right up, or I'll stick a pin in you."

VIEW OF BUILDINGS FROM THE EAST.
Zarephath Academy (Pillar of Fire), Zarephath, N. J.

Zarephath in a 1920s postcard photo. *Author's collection.*

THIS IS AN INVITATION TO VISIT....

Zarephath, New Jersey
PILLAR of FIRE---NATIONAL HEADQUARTERS

Come on Sunday and spend the day—hear Bishop Alma White. Three public services are held—11 a.m. and 3 p.m. in the church auditorium on the Campus, and in the Fillar of Fire Temple, Main Street, Bound Brook, in the evening at 7 o'clock.

ALMA WHITE
Founder

These services are broadcast. Old-time religion and current world events are discussed by Bishop Alma White and other Pillar of Fire preachers.

If you cannot arrange to be present on Sunday, visit us during the week.

Pipe Organ, Orchestra, Pillar of Fire Band

Here are located *Alma White College, Alma Preparatory School, Zarephath Bible Seminary*. Send for catalogs. **(OVER)**

ZAREPHATH, N. J.
National headquarters of the Pillar of Fire and home of Station WAWZ

A card inviting people to come and hear Alma. *Author's collection.*

White was described as a leader of great versatility who lived by the motto "Do it now." She was also enmeshed in prejudicial beliefs, however, and fervently supported the Ku Klux Klan.

White formed a close relationship with Arthur Bell, a rising star of the New Jersey Klan. Bell wrote introductions to her books and allegedly wrote a book of his own, entitled *The Ku Klux Klan or the Knights of Columbus Klan: America or Rome*—an anti-Catholic piece that gained popularity in Klan circles—although White may have been the actual author.

A recruiting representative of the Klan, known as a kleagle, visited the Pillar of Fire Church on May 1, 1923, no doubt with the belief that it would prove a fertile recruiting ground. Unfortunately for him, word of his appearance got out to the larger community around Bound Brook, and a mob of anti-Klan locals gathered at the venue. The original intent of the protestors seems to have been to heckle the Klan speaker, whose opening statement enthusiastically described the revived Klan as the "most remarkable movement of modern times."

The intense hissing and booing that ensued was the first major hostile public reaction to the Klan in New Jersey. The atmosphere deteriorated, and the meeting turned into a riot in which twenty-five cars were damaged and one hundred "Holy Jumpers" ended up besieged in the "Fiery Temple" under a barrage of stones. Local police and state troopers got the situation under control.

A reporter noticed there was a good deal of Alma White's literature scattered around the scene of the disturbance, including a pamphlet entitled "Ku Klux Klan and Woman's Cause," based on an address she had made the previous December, which praised the Klan as "the prophets of a new and better age." In what seems to be a characteristic silence regarding the Ku Klux Klan in many New Jersey histories, an account of religion in the state published in 1964 makes no mention of the Klan or Alma White's connection to it. The account merely notes that White was "a prolific writer, penning many books, magazines, pamphlets and brochures," which were "in large measure responsible for the securing of funds" for her religious colony.

Despite growing public opposition to the Klan, the rancor did not seem to affect White's success. In the years that followed the 1923 disturbance, she continued to build an empire that included schools, two colleges and two non-commercial radio stations. She toured the country for years and embarked on fifty-eight trips overseas, including voyages to Egypt and Palestine. White was joined in her efforts by her two sons, Arthur and Ray, both ordained ministers who played key roles in the organization.

White's husband, Kent, died in 1940. The indomitable Alma White lived for six more years, but even she could not stop the inevitable assault of age. The last year of her life was marred by failing health, and she died at home in 1946. She was eighty-four.

When asked at the height of her career what her church represented, White replied, "We stand for a vital Christianity that means holiness in living." White's sect was unrelenting in its fight against cards, the theater, dancing, smoking and liquor. Unfortunately, White and her followers were also adamant in their stance against African Americans, Catholics and numerous other groups. Her rigid belief system was tainted by a bitter undercurrent of intolerance, which has irrevocably tarnished and diminished her religious legacy.

ARTHUR BELL

New Jersey's Grand Dragon

He staged racist rallies, shook hands with Nazis and helped create an unsavory enclave at the Jersey Shore that promoted the ideals of white privilege and superiority. Arthur Hornbui Bell immersed himself in the nefarious underworld of the Ku Klux Klan, and for a brief time, he helped build an empire that struck fear in the hearts of African Americans, Jews, Catholics, immigrants and other groups targeted by the notorious hate group.

Born in New York in 1891, Bell began his career innocuously enough as a vaudevillian who, with his wife, Leah, combined a song and dance act with ventriloquism. During World War I, the duo served overseas as YMCA entertainers for the army. Upon returning home, the Bells were swept up in the tumultuous postwar era that threatened conservative Americans with its emphasis on emancipated women, bootleg booze, a new wave of immigrants and political unrest.

Fueled by fear and prejudice, the Ku Klux Klan began its ascent to power and notoriety. The white supremacist hate group was first established in the wake of the Civil War and was suppressed through federal intervention. The second Klan was founded in 1915, inspired by the D.W. Griffith film *The Birth of a Nation*, which romanticized the original Klan's founding.

Bell sensed an opportunity with the growing Klan and used his influence to create a more visible and theatrical presence for the organization in New Jersey. In October 1922, in an abandoned quarry between Bernardsville and Summit, he staged a public "naturalization," Klanspeak for initiation ceremony, of two hundred candidates from nine New Jersey cities. Reporters and photographers were advised that while they could not actually attend the ceremony, they would be able to observe it from the edge of the quarry.

Following the dramatic event, Bell's rise to power was swift, and by the following year, he had been anointed the "Grand Titan" in charge of the central New Jersey Klan. Continuing his quest to highlight Klan activity and influence, Bell invited a reporter to an initiation ceremony in Allenwood. The affair, no doubt carefully orchestrated, featured a circle of cars, their headlights directed at an altar and cross in the middle of a field in which an estimated 750 Klansmen chanted as 300 initiates filed into the circle. The ceremony ended with everyone kneeling to pray as the cross burst into flames.

By 1924, Bell had become even more ambitious and planned a massive public event for the Fourth of July weekend. Bell needed a suitably impressive venue, which came about through the efforts of two Klan representatives, who negotiated a deal to purchase the Elkwood Park property in Long Branch, today the site of Monmouth Park racetrack. By late June, the *New York Times* reported, the site had become crowded with mechanics and laborers "transforming the 130-acre tract into a place for the reception of thousands of visitors."

Although the theme of the scheduled festivities was ostensibly "religious and political freedom," it turned into a "Krusade" against Irish Catholic New York governor Alfred E. Smith, who was viewed as a potential Democratic presidential candidate in 1924. The crowd "howlingly endorsed" a speaker's declaration that "no one but a Protestant will ever sit in the White House." Although Bell would later deny it, there was apparently a carnival game in which customers could "hurl balls at an effigy of Governor Smith."

The highlight of the event was an afternoon march down Broadway, Long Branch's main thoroughfare. The parade was led by a mounted robed Klansman with a green sash and featured three bands and floats from a dozen Monmouth County towns. The sidewalks along the line of the march were packed with spectators, both supporters and opponents, who were generally orderly save for an occasional firecracker.

The merchants of Long Branch were not happy with the aftermath of the Klonvocation, according to a 1940 retrospective: "The Jewish summer residents departed from the town the next day, practically en masse, leaving a deserted city of ruined shopkeepers and empty hotels and boarding houses." African Americans and Catholics either left the city or temporarily sequestered themselves.

In the months that followed, Bell's ascent in the Klan hierarchy was threatened by a series of scandals that undermined the Klan's already dubious reputation.

The beleaguered Bell attempted to soften the Klan's image with a Mother's Day rally in the Methodist "camp meeting" and vacation town of Ocean Grove. On May 11, 1925, an estimated eight thousand people, including a "large representation of Klan members from various parts of the state," attended the ceremony in the massive Great Auditorium. The Elkwood Park Klan band performed on the stage in full regalia, and a soloist crooned "Mother of Mine." The audience sang "The Old Rugged Cross" and filed out as the Klan Band played "Onward, Christian Soldiers."

Bell and Leah returned to the Ocean Grove Auditorium on July 19 to address another large crowd "almost entirely of Klan members or sympathizers" on the topic of "the flag and the American home and the Bible." Bell likened the Klan to a "militant army for Christ" and compared the women of the Klan to Betsy Ross in their dedication to the country and its flag. Responding to calls for Klansmen to unmask, Bell answered, "The Ku Klux Klan will consider removing their masks when crooked politicians remove the masks from their souls."

Despite his concerted efforts at spreading Klan propaganda, Bell's machinations continued to be challenged by negative publicity. He once again took to the defensive as he dealt with a suicide note that suggested Klan involvement. John Sampson of Port Monmouth, who in September 1925 shot himself in the heart while in a car at Sea Bright and left a vague note that blamed the Klan for his self-administered demise.

Sampson was allegedly a partner in a roadside stand that was "said to be jointly owned by the Ku Klux Klan organizations of Keyport, Keansburg and Belford." Bell successfully stifled the story with a quick disavowal of Sampson's membership in the organization.

Because of his ability to grow the Klan and its influence in spite of a somewhat rocky road in New Jersey, Bell was designated the first grand dragon of New Jersey during a lavish ceremony at Elkwood Park on March 17, 1926. The one thousand Klansmen present burned a cross at midnight in celebration and showered him with gifts.

Every demagogue needs a suitable base of operations, and Bell found his at the sprawling Klan headquarters in Wall Township, known as the Monmouth Pleasure Club. A promotional brochure for the site described the land in lush, idyllic terms as a scenic site with "an unobstructed view of river and sea." The grounds were dominated by a stately hotel, which was constructed for the previous tenant, the Marconi Belmar Receiving Station. It had originally functioned as a housing headquarters for staff at the former international communications center.

It was no secret that the Klan's exclusionary ideals would be implemented at its new headquarters or that the Monmouth Pleasure Club was a business front for the group or at least its local membership.

Under Bell's aegis, the property became the site of a dizzying whirlwind of social activities, including a weeklong circus and a three-day Fourth of July celebration in 1926. To promote the July event, it was announced that "an American flag would fly from a balloon during the celebration, and Klan officials have declared that this will be visible for twenty miles."

The festivities began Saturday evening with a grand ball and reception and concluded Monday with speeches, a band concert, a parade and the burning of the "Old Fiery Cross" at eleven o'clock at night. The elaborate celebration was yet another calculated theatrical effort by Bell "to impress upon thousands of visitors to the north Jersey shore resorts the strength of the hooded organization," according to a local news report. The three-day celebration was interpreted as an effort to widely advertise the Shark River reservation as a potential resort for Klansmen and members of affiliated organizations.

The opulent event's success was marred, however, by bickering between Klan activists and Klan real estate entrepreneurs. Klan activists claimed that the resort was Klan property, while the deed holders, who happened to be local Klansmen, asserted that the headquarters property was merely leased to the organization.

By 1927, the dispute had become a bitter wrangle acted out in highly publicized court proceedings. Bell was in the forefront of the fight for the Klan, working out of his living quarters in a comfortable bungalow at the resort. The contentious Klan leader continued to make local headlines, particularly after an unfortunate reporter asked him to discuss the Klan's position on the land dispute. The grand dragon responded that he had no comment on the case and casually added that he was carrying a gun, asking whether the reporter was afraid. The intrepid interviewer responded that he was not frightened and was more interested in learning about recent developments in the property battle. Bell refused to provide any details.

The land dispute worked its way through a labyrinth of court battles, culminating in a U.S. Circuit Court of Appeals decision that the Klan's contention of ownership was not based on any actual evidence.

The career of Grand Dragon Bell paralleled the failing fortunes of the Klan, despite his continuing reputation for a "fiery tongue and boastful speeches." In April 1928, after the aggressive huckster fought so vigorously for possession of the Pleasure Club property, Bell suffered the ultimate indignity: eviction from his "comfortable cottage" on the estate. Bell and his wife ended up in a West Belmar apartment following their ouster.

Bell's days of popularity and political influence seemed over, and it was probably not a shocking news development when he resigned from his Klan leadership position in 1929. The *Asbury Park Press* noted that Bell's "power began to wane about two years ago" when the legal battle with the Pleasure Club began. The case indeed initiated the unraveling of Bell's Klan career, and Bell and Leah returned to Bloomfield, where he reportedly opened a lunchroom.

There may have been more to Bell's resignation than met the public eye. In 1930, thirty-five-year-old Leah Bell moved back to her parents' home in Grand Rapids, Michigan, and shortly thereafter filed for divorce on grounds of "cruelty." Arthur Bell did not contest the divorce, which was granted on August 28, 1930. It was kept from the public until November, when Arthur married twenty-two-year-old Florence Kierstead, a secretary who had worked for him for several years.

Bell had returned to rabble-rousing by the time of his marriage to Florence. He had a new partner, William J. Simmons, founder of the second iteration of the Klan, who recruited Bell into his new organization, the Caucasian Crusaders of the White Band, subsequently shortened to the White Band.

Simmons's group dropped the anti-Catholic and Jewish tropes of the Klan and opened membership to all white males over the age of eighteen. The group fed on the increasing anxiety of Americans, caused in no part by the beginning of the Great Depression. In such an atmosphere, it was easy to exploit race and point to African Americans and Asians as the cause of job loss by white men.

Bell became the organization's "Superintending Ambassador" for New Jersey, but the hate group failed to gain traction and media mention of him all but vanished. The occasional single-line notice in the *Asbury Park Press* noted that a friend from the shore was visiting him in Bloomfield.

Not one to be content with staying out of the public limelight, Bell resurfaced in the Klan by the late 1930s, when changing internal politics gave him the opportunity to reclaim some of his former power and influence. Under Bell's leadership, the Klan persisted in maintaining a somewhat visible presence in New Jersey, despite increasingly stiff opposition. When thirty Klan members, led by Bell in a golden robe, gathered on February 12,

1940, in Wanaque, they were greeted by the "boos of milling townsfolk" and were pelted with eggs as they left the meeting.

The Klan's admiration of Nazi Germany intensified throughout the 1930s and culminated in a joint rally that proved disastrous for the New Jersey branch and Bell. The rally was held in conjunction with the German American Bund, an American version of the Nazi Party whose members dressed in Nazi-style uniforms and gave one another fascist salutes. The leader of the Bund during the height of its power in the late 1930s was Fritz Kuhn, a swaggering Munich-born chemist and World War I German army veteran who demanded absolute obedience from his followers.

Public tolerance in New Jersey had become shaky by the time the Bund and Klan held their joint rally on August 18, 1940. Nearly two hundred Klansmen and several hundred of their friends and relatives were met at Camp Nordland by some eight hundred Bundsmen and were "graciously escorted around the grounds by storm troopers dressed in black trousers, white shirts and black ties." Bundsman August Klapprott and Bell met on a platform and "smilingly shook hands." Klan members expressed sympathy for members of the Bund, who they asserted "had been persecuted" for their adherence to the doctrines of Nazi Germany.

Toward the end of the rally, a crowd of about five hundred Sussex County residents "gathered at the camp gate and intermittently attempted to drown out proceedings by singing the Star-Spangled Banner." The fury intensified in the following days when national Klan officials expressed their dismay over the joint rally and ousted Bell from the organization. A top Klan member alleged that Bell permitted a "high officer of the German American Bund" to address the gathering and that Bell "failed to live up to the ideals of the Klan" in his management of the assembly. Klan leadership contended that there could be "no sympathy" between the Bund and Klan.

The Klan endured mounting scrutiny and public hostility following the rally debacle, particularly since its message of divisiveness threatened the pressing demand for national unity during the war years. After a secret Klonvocation was held in April 1944, Imperial Wizard James Colescott announced the Klan had disbanded as a national organization. Following the defeat of the Axis powers, however, the Klan once again insinuated itself into the political scene.

After the war, rumors of a Klan resurgence in New Jersey were squelched when Governor Walter Edge asked his attorney general to propose the Klan be outlawed as "an organization destructive of the rights and liberties of the

Arthur Bell (*left*) flirts with Nazi August Klapprott. *Author's collection.*

people" and that its 1923 incorporation papers in the state be revoked. The New Jersey Supreme Court granted that request in 1946.

By now, Bell was doubting the feasibility of a Klan resurgence, telling an inquiring journalist that "the Klan is dead beyond recognition." He envisioned a place for "an organization along Klan lines, but it must be carefully organized, embracing this time the Catholic and Jew, as well as the Protestant." African Americans, he suggested, "should be placed in an auxiliary."

Despite occasional flareups, the Klan—and Bell's relevance—steadily declined. For Bell, the boisterous and bigoted showman, the descent into anonymity and public indifference was undoubtedly a bitter reckoning. He died in obscurity in 1971, a forgotten relic from an infamous chapter in New Jersey history.

DR. HENRY COTTON

Psychiatric Surgeon

W elcome to the Trenton State Hospital, ma'am. My name is Dr. Henry Cotton, and I run this place. They tell me you feel very depressed. We have a cure for that. First, we shall extract several of your teeth, and if it persists, we shall remove your tonsils, and there is always the option of a hysterectomy. Do not worry, most of our patients, although I do not have the exact number, survive."

One of the things we loved about the HBO series *Boardwalk Empire* was that, aside from the exaggeration of Nucky's behavior for dramatic purposes, many of the other characters were real people of the era, and the actors played the parts in a historically accurate manner and, in some cases, even physically resembled the original people.

Toward the end of the series, the character Gillian Darmody was committed to Trenton State Hospital, formerly the New Jersey State Lunatic Asylum, seen in the accompanying late nineteenth-century image. In the series, the state hospital was a mental institution run by a "Dr. Cotton," who was Henry Andrews Cotton, a psychiatrist born in 1876 in Norfolk, Virginia, who was indeed the medical director of the Trenton State Hospital between 1907 and 1930.

Cotton's credentials were impressive. He had studied medicine at Johns Hopkins University under Dr. Adolf Meyer, the best-known psychiatrist of the early twentieth century, and then in Europe under the auspices of some of the most prominent psychiatrists of the day, then often referred to as "alienists."

New Jersey Lunatic Asylum. *Author's collection.*

Dr. Cotton was an enthusiastic proponent of the "surgical bacteriology" theory, which posited that mental disorders were the result of infections in the body and that there was, therefore, a surgical cure for them. In 1921, he wrote a book on his theories titled *The Defective Delinquent and Insane; The Relation of Focal Infections to Their Causation, Treatment and Prevention*, which, despite its pedantic academic title, was highly regarded.

The concept was not entirely new. In the mid-nineteenth century, when women were often committed to asylums by their husbands for not conforming to their perceived gender roles as subservient housewives, surgery to remove certain body parts, including ovaries and clitoris, was often prescribed by alienists as a cure. Hysteria was considered a female disease.

In 1915, Cotton, claiming that his institution was "no longer an asylum nor custodial institution but is to be looked upon as a curative institution or hospital in every sense of the word," addressed the annual convention of New Jersey physicians in the Jersey Shore town of Spring Lake. His subject was the treatment of paresis and locomotor ataxia (a condition of paralysis and dementia in the later stages of syphilis) and curing those ailments through speedy treatment at his hospital. He maintained that such treatment, which he did not elaborate on, was highly effective, resulting in a 35.5 percent complete cure and a 22 percent improvement rate.

Cotton and his staff would begin treatment by extracting the teeth of a mental patient, then moving on to tonsils and other organs, including testicles and ovaries, the latter the treatment applied to Gillian in *Boardwalk Empire*. In the pre-antibiotic era, such surgeries could have drastic results, and Cotton did admit to a 30 percent death rate in his patients, although a later analysis proved it was closer to 45 percent. Ironically, he was in other ways a progressive, abolished mandatory restraints for patients and had regular staff meetings to discuss issues.

Dr. Cotton. *Wikimedia Commons.*

In 1921, Mrs. Georgeanna Phillips of Ocean Grove, a discharged patient, claimed that Cotton had authorized surgery on her without her permission. The type of surgery was not specified, but a newspaper declared that it "was said that the operation would bar her from motherhood." Dr. Cotton replied that the operation performed was to "benefit her mental condition." The charge was dismissed.

Perhaps surprisingly to many today, Cotton got a lot of support from professionals in the field. The *New York Times* also endorsed him, declaring in 1922 that his New Jersey hospital was "the most progressive institution in the world for the care of the insane" due to his "brilliant leadership."

Despite all the praise, Cotton's theories were becoming controversial in some medical circles. Dr. Phyllis Greenacre, who was assigned to investigate his work by his former mentor, Dr. Meyer at Johns Hopkins, later described Cotton as a "singularly peculiar" individual and noted that when she tried to interview patients at his hospital, they were often unintelligible because all their teeth had been removed. The criticism of Greenacre and some other doctors led to a New Jersey state senate committee, led by Senator William Bright, investigating alleged waste of taxpayer money at the state hospital and other complaints regarding patient treatment at the institution in 1925. Cotton became emotionally ill during the hearing, expressing fear to one of his subordinates that he would be arrested. Some speculated that he had a "nervous breakdown." He diagnosed his problem as caused by infected teeth, had several pulled and then declared himself cured.

One question raised by the committee was the release of sixty-four-year-old Aretta Quackenbush of Tennant, in Monmouth County, whom Cotton had released from the state hospital and who, upon returning home, killed her "feeble minded daughter" Gladys. Cotton maintained that he had not removed her teeth or tonsils because of her age and that the tragedy was the fault of her sister and brother-in-law, who insisted on her release and housed her with her daughter. Senator Simpson asked Cotton, "Did you know you were discharging a homicidal maniac?" Cotton answered that she showed no signs of such a malady while she was in his hospital. Simpson and the other legislators went on to question hospital financial matters, such as who was paying Dr. Greenacre. In the end, Cotton was neither fired nor arrested, and he continued his work.

Henry Andrews Cotton retired as medical director of the hospital in 1930 and died of a heart attack in 1933, but not before opining to the press as "an internationally known alienist" that Giuseppe Zangara, who had tried to assassinate President-elect Franklin D. Roosevelt, was incited to do so due to "stomach pains," apparently a not uncommon ailment for mentally deranged presidential assassins. Cotton was posthumously lauded by journalists as a pioneering figure in American mental health treatment. Thankfully, psychiatric care progressed after his demise. For the complete and detailed account of Dr. Cotton and his career, we recommend Andrew Scull's book, *Madhouse: A Tragic Tale of Megalomania and Modern Medicine.*

DORIS BRADWAY

New Jersey's First Woman Mayor

Doris Mohan was born on October 31, 1895, in Elizabeth, New Jersey, and "was educated at Miss Spence's seminary near that city, attended business college in Philadelphia and studied vocal music in Europe." In 1919, she married Edwin Tomlinson Bradway and moved to Wildwood, New Jersey.

As Doris Bradway, she become involved in local politics and was appointed as Wildwood's city finance commissioner in August 1932 to replace Kenneth K. Kirby, who was killed in an auto accident. The mother of two was reportedly the "first woman commissioner in the east." The reporter was quick to add, however, in case any men got nervous, that "she takes care of her household tasks by rising earlier in the morning."

Bradway organized the Bradway Ladies' Republican Club, promising that "when their wishes were not observed," her 309 lady members would vote for Democrats. In response, Richard Gownly suggested an opposing male organization, leading one reporter to speculate that Gownly "may have started a veritable 'war of the sexes'" in Cape May County. Gownly was quoted as saying, "Politics is a man's job. No more minding the baby while they go to political meetings." Bradway replied, "We can do more with a bit of lipstick than all the neckties in the world...we will humor them. Men are such children anyway."

On August 29, 1933, following the death of Wildwood mayor William H. Bright, the remaining two commissioners, no doubt considering her lady voters, appointed Bradway as mayor, making her the first woman

Mayor Bradway. *Author's collection.*

mayor in New Jersey history. Her first official act was to marry a vacationing couple from Willow Grove, Pennsylvania. Shortly after her installation, Police Chief Oakford M. Cobb accused Bradway of instructing his officers "to keep out of pool rooms, cabarets and saloons and other public places," as well as of hiring private investigators to enforce her edict on the department. In response, the New Jersey Supreme Court ordered an investigation of the Wildwood municipal conflict.

The story was that the establishments the police were forbidden to enter had illegal slot machines. The presence of slot machines in Wildwood did not, however, begin with the Bradway administration. During the investigative hearings, liquor dealer Edward Meyers testified that he had once paid the deceased politicians Kirby and Bright $1,000 for a four-year slot machine monopoly. The most recent Wildwood slot baron was hotelier Andrew Applegate. Chief Cobb stated, somewhat dubiously, that he was unaware of slot machines and Applegate's role but that the new mayor was providing free gasoline to the hotel owner at city expense.

The chief was seemingly contradicted by Martin Long, one of his patrolmen, who testified that he had not only reported the gambling devices but had also won $1.50 on one. There were other troubling revelations as well. Witness Samuel Garrigues of Blackwood testified that he had to make a $150 campaign donation to Bradway to receive a Wildwood taxi license. Another witness stated that Bradway's cook, Cassie Turner, operated an unlicensed saloon.

In the wake of the investigation, a special prosecutor was appointed, and in August 1935, Mayor Bradway was accused of malfeasance in office and went to trial. Numerous character witnesses defended the mayor, and her attorney called the charges "a challenge to the womanhood of the country." Two police officers testified that they had not seen evidence of slot machines since she was elected. She was acquitted by the jury.

There was more to come in the story of Mayor Doris Bradway. Following her reelection in 1936, Bradway's husband was accused of "aiding and abetting" voter fraud by paying Philadelphia ne'er-do-well "floater voter"

Harold D. Grossen to vote several times for the Republican senate candidate in an election for the state legislature.

By December 1937, Mayor Bradway was under fire again after a legislative committee accused her administration of being "corrupt, selfish and unthinking." According to the legislators, she, as well as her deceased predecessor, had "loaded the city payroll" in return for bribes, among other things. Bradway's response was that any offenses she committed were unintentional and due to her lack of understanding of the law. The committee reported that "she tried to excuse her woeful lack of knowledge by insisting that she was 'dumb—yes, very dumb'—and that…the transition from housewife to manager of the fiscal affairs of the City of Wildwood was much too great." They noted as well that she was, in fact, well versed in the business of governance.

Bradway claimed that the investigation, like the previous one, was a "partisan affair," launched by Democratic legislators (Republicans refused to participate), adding that she was sure Democratic boss and mayor of Jersey City Frank Hague was behind the accusations. A newspaper summed up the matter by declaring, "Politics as it is played in Cape May County sometimes has a smell somewhat akin to the back bay at low tide. They float other things than oysters down there."

Although the investigation did not lead to charges, Doris Bradway lost her position in a 1938 recall election, but she remained active in Wildwood politics and made the newspapers for the rest of her life. In 1941, she divorced Edwin, claiming that he was "indifferent to her," and in 1943 married Fred Nathaniel. In 1956, she announced her candidacy once more but backed out before the election.

In 1966, after serving as violations clerk for the city court over the summer tourist season, Bradway denied accusations that the town had not picked up trash on the boardwalk, stating, "We had to contend with human trash. I've never seen anything like it. Fifteen-year-old boys and girls were involved in drinking and had to be dragged off the boardwalk by police. That is what I object to, that kind of trash—not paper and other items."

New Jersey's first woman mayor died at Burdette Tomlin Memorial Hospital in Cape May Courthouse on March 30, 1982, at the age of eighty-six.

MARY TERESA NORTON

The First New Jersey Congresswoman

Mary Teresa Norton was born Mary Teresa Hopkins in Jersey City to Irish immigrant parents in 1875. She attended a local parochial elementary school. Some accounts of her life assert that she graduated from Dickinson High School, then known as Jersey City High School, but others are vague about her education, noting that she "pursued an informal education at home" with the assistance of her brother James, who the family intended to become a Catholic priest but who eventually became the principal of Jersey City High School and then superintendent of schools for Jersey City.

Mary's mother died when she was seventeen, and she and her two sisters moved to New York City when her father remarried in 1896. They attended Packard Business College in the city, where they acquired clerical skills and shared an apartment.

In 1909, Mary married Francis Norton, a widower with two children. The following year, she had a child, Robert, who died shortly after his birth. In part no doubt to assuage her sorrow, Ms. Norton began working at the Queen's Daughters Day Nursery, rising to become the organization's secretary and then president in 1916. She was the nursery's major fundraiser and, during World War I, also organized a Red Cross workroom for women in the St. Joseph parish hall basement. Her social work enabled Norton to meet a considerable number of influential people in politics, including Frank Hague, who became Jersey City's mayor in 1917 and would go on to be New Jersey's most powerful political boss.

Hague noticed and was impressed by Norton's enthusiasm and fundraising abilities and, as women's ability to vote became a reality, recruited her into the state's Democratic Party in 1921. The mayor reportedly told Norton, "It's your duty to organize the women of Jersey City."

Norton soon became the first New Jersey female Democratic Committee member and then, in 1923, was elected the first Democratic woman freeholder (today a commissioner) in New Jersey on the Hudson County Board of Freeholders. Noticing that the infant mortality rate in Hudson County in 1923 was 212 per 1,000 births, she successfully obtained board approval and funding for the construction of a maternity hospital in Jersey City at county expense, a special project of "Boss" Hague and named after his mother, Margaret.

Norton, encouraged by Hague, ran for the Twelfth New Jersey District (Jersey City and Bayonne) seat in the U.S. Congress in 1924 and won in a landslide with 62 percent of the vote, the first female Democrat and first New Jersey woman to serve in Congress. She was eager to get started and went down to Washington several months before she would assume the position of, as one newspaper called her, a "Congressman" to investigate possible committee assignments.

Norton was particularly interested in care for veterans of the "World War" and "reducing taxes for working people," who, she declared, were "the backbone of the Nation." During her five terms as chair of the Committee on Labor, Norton introduced and pursued policies to improve working conditions across the country. After her initial bill to reduce taxes failed, she said, "We can give relief to our foreign debtors; why cannot we extend similar relief to the people at home, the taxpayers of the greatest Nation in the world?" She was more successful in her goal of funding the establishment of a veterans hospital in New Jersey.

When Franklin D. Roosevelt won the presidency and assumed the job in early 1932, Mary Norton was immediately classified as a "New Dealer" and, in a Democrat-controlled House of Representatives, introduced legislation to repeal the Eighteenth Amendment and end Prohibition.

Throughout her years in the House of Representatives, which lasted until her retirement in 1951, Norton became the chairperson of three Congressional committees—Veterans Affairs, the District of Columbia and Labor—and, in the latter position, sponsored legislation to establish a minimum wage rate for workers engaged in interstate commerce. Her career was distinguished by service and loyalty to her party and her constituents, and she would become the most prominent Democrat in New Jersey, aside from Hague.

Left: Mary Norton packs her bag to go home after a successful season in the New Deal Congress in 1938. *Author's collection.*

Below: Mary Norton and fellow congresswomen celebrate her twenty-six years in Congress in 1950. *Author's collection.*

During World War II, Norton fought for equal pay for women in the workplace and successfully advocated for government-sponsored daycare centers for working women, likely due to her own history as a volunteer worker in Jersey City, where she saw the problems of working women with children. A constant advocate for her gender, she also had an interest in legislation affecting working-class men. When a congressman addressed her as a "lady," Norton replied, "I am no lady, I'm a Member of Congress, and I'll proceed on that basis."

Norton was characterized by some at the time and since as being simply a servant of Mayor Hague, whom she called her "political foster father."

While her ideas were certainly comparable in many ways to the mayor's, she did what she did to help her constituents and was an effective representative of their needs.

Over the course of her career, Congresswoman Norton was awarded several honors. Mayor Hague proclaimed a "Mary Norton Day" in Jersey City in the summer of 1942. She was publicly honored at Roosevelt Stadium and received a gold watch as well as praise from the mayor for her legislative achievements.

In 1951, after twenty-six years in Congress, seventy-five-year-old Mary Norton retired, four years after Frank Hague completed his final term as mayor of Jersey City. A widow, she moved from Jersey City to Greenwich, Connecticut, close to her sister, where she died at age eighty-four in August 1959.

While Norton is not remembered by many modern New Jerseyans, she still maintains a presence in Jersey City. Hudson County Community College has named a conference room in her honor, and the Mary Norton Manor, a housing project, stands on Duncan Avenue in the city. There was also a national reminder. During Women's History Month in 2001, then Congressional minority leader Nancy Pelosi hung a portrait of Norton in her office.

DONALD W. McGOWAN

The State's Finest Soldier

One of our favorite New Jersey soldiers, Donald W. McGowan was born in 1899 in Orange, New Jersey. In 1916, he enlisted in Company I of the New Jersey National Guard's 5th Infantry Regiment. McGowan went to the Mexican border when the National Guard was mobilized in the wake of Pancho Villa's raid on Columbus, New Mexico. Called back to the colors for World War I, he rose to the rank of battalion sergeant major in the 114th Infantry Regiment at the age of nineteen.

After the war, McGowan was selected to attend West Point but left the academy after several months, returned home and was commissioned as a second lieutenant in the New Jersey National Guard. Over the succeeding years, he rose to the rank of lieutenant colonel and served as assistant adjutant general of the state's National Guard from 1936 to 1941. Promoted to colonel, McGowan was placed in command of the New Jersey National Guard's 102nd Cavalry, a "horse-mechanized" unit that still had one squadron mounted on horseback, when the unit was called to active duty for a year of training at Fort Jackson, South Carolina, in January 1941. The colonel addressed the thousand men of his new command before they left by train from Newark for the South, telling them, "You will be training against the day we may be in battle against a power that is yet to be defeated."

McGowan, described by a newspaper as "Dashing Donald McGowan," led the 102nd in training and maneuvers prior to the United States' entry into World War II. After Pearl Harbor, the 102nd was retained in service for the remainder of the war. It was the first of the state's National Guard

Above: Private McGowan in 1915. *Courtesy of John J. McGowan.*

Opposite: Colonel McGowan (*at left*) and officers of the 102nd Cavalry at Fort Jackson, South Carolina, in 1941. *Courtesy of NGMMNJ.*

units to deploy overseas, traveling to England in 1942. One squadron was subsequently shipped from England to North Africa, where it became the guard unit for diplomats and other VIPs. That squadron was re-designated as the 117th Cavalry Squadron and later fought in Italy. The remainder of the regiment, now named the 102nd Cavalry Group, reinforced by a squadron of draftees to replace the 117th, was led ashore by Colonel McGowan at Normandy on D-Day Plus 2.

Noted for looking out for his men's welfare, McGowan complained to a senior officer over what he considered to be an inappropriate mission for his unit and was relieved of command of the 102nd and reassigned as provost marshal for the Normandy Sector, which included a massive POW camp. McGowan was cited by a postwar journalist as "a guardian angel for the welfare of young men. These have included young German POWs." McGowan said, "It was there I learned to delegate authority and quit worrying." Meanwhile, his well-trained 102nd Cavalry would be the first American unit to move into Paris. Interestingly, the 117th Squadron was the first American unit to move into Rome.

Following the war. McGowan returned to New Jersey, where he resumed his position as assistant adjutant general and then as commander of the New Jersey National Guard 50th Armored Division's Combat Command

General McGowan at his desk in Washington, D.C. *Courtesy of John McGowan.*

B in 1946. He was promoted to brigadier general in 1947 and served as deputy chief of staff of the New Jersey National Guard. Promoted to major general in 1948, McGowan was appointed to command the 50th Armored Division by Governor Alfred Driscoll, one of the state's finest governors, succeeding Major General Clifford Powell, who had been relieved by the governor following his involvement in a real estate scam scheme.

In nominating McGowan, Governor Driscoll said, "General McGowan has served in the New Jersey National Guard since his enlistment in 1916, during which period he has been in federal service three times, passing successively through the noncommissioned and commissioned ranks to his present rank and served overseas in both wars. His wartime service and his superior performance of duty in the organization of the postwar National Guard successively as commanding general of Combat Command A and Combat Command B warrant his promotion to major general." McGowan was subsequently praised for "molding New Jersey's 50th Armored Division into one of the very top units in the United States."

In November 1955, McGowan went to Washington to become chief of the army branch of the National Guard Bureau and, in July 1959, was appointed by President Eisenhower as chief of the entire National Guard Bureau. A reporter, writing on the strength of the American military in December 1961, spoke of McGowan as "a doggedly exacting, persistent but kindly, Major General."

Major General McGowan retired in 1963, the last soldier still on active duty who had deployed to the Mexican border in 1916. He died in 1967 and was buried at Arlington National Cemetery.

TESSIE McNAMARA

Heroine of Lyndhurst

New Jersey had been a developing industrial state for many years, but according to one account, "the guns of Europe" that sounded in World War I were responsible for "the most intense industrialization in its history." The production of high explosives, textiles, steel and ships rocketed to new heights. The Bureau of Statistics reported that expansion in manufacturing was 400 percent greater in 1916 than in any preceding year. The chemical industry in New Jersey sprang up almost overnight. Six factories to produce aniline, formerly imported from Germany, were set up within the state, the most important at Kearny. Another source states that the state's overall industrial output "increased almost 300 percent between 1914 and 1919." By 1917, New Jersey was the largest ammunition-producing state in the country, with all of that production going to Great Britain, France and Russia. Unfortunately, this industrial expansion also made New Jersey a target.

On July 30, 1916, the "Black Tom" ammunition pier on the Hudson River in Jersey City exploded. The force of the explosion broke windows all over Jersey City and Manhattan and damaged the Statue of Liberty, as well as buildings on the nearby Ellis Island immigration station. Damage in Jersey City alone was estimated at $1 million ($23 million in today's money). Large amounts of ammunition manufactured in the United States were shipped to the Allies in Europe through Jersey City and Hoboken, and it was believed that German saboteurs had placed bombs on the pier. Six months after Black Tom, another suspicious massive explosion occurred across the

The explosion at Kingsland continues into the night. *Author's collection.*

meadowlands just over seven miles away in Kingsland, an area of Lyndhurst, at a forty-acre ammunition manufacturing plant operated by the Canadian Car and Foundry Company.

In the late afternoon of January 11, 1917, a fire broke out at a worker's bench in a building that prepared shells for cleaning and loading and quickly spread throughout the plant buildings, as well as to nearby ammunition-filled railroad cars waiting to leave for Jersey City for shipment to Russia. The fire initiated an hours-long daisy chain of explosions as hundreds of thousands of shells either detonated or were thrown into the air, causing more than $17 million of damage.

Twenty-five-year-old telephone operator (or, as they called them then, "hello girl") Theresa "Tessie" McNamara, the first woman hired by the company, became a heroine that day. Tessie spotted a column of smoke coming from a shed near an explosive storage area and knew what the consequences of that would be, but she stayed at her post, calling not only the fire and police departments but all forty buildings in the complex as well, warning workers to evacuate immediately as the explosions reached a crescendo that rained shrapnel on the roof a few feet over her head and shook windows in upper Manhattan.

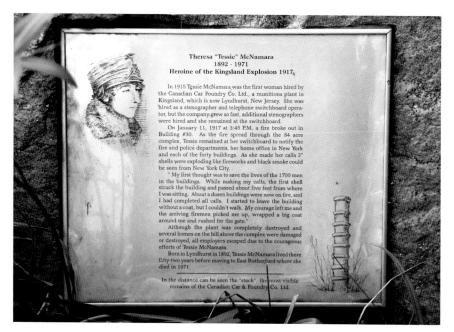

Tessie's memorial. *Courtesy of Jim Madden.*

Tessie McNamara's subsequent account of her actions that day is a testament to her courage: "My first thought was to save the lives of the 1,700 men in the buildings. While making my calls, the first shell struck the building and passed about five feet from where I was sitting. About a dozen buildings were now on fire, and I had completed all calls. I started to leave the building without a coat, but I couldn't walk. My courage left me, and the arriving firemen picked me up, wrapped a big coat around me and rushed for the gate."

The plant was destroyed, and the houses overlooking it from a nearby hill, many of them occupied by the company's largely immigrant workforce, were damaged or destroyed. Several homes in neighboring Rutherford were struck by flying shells, and a car the police chiefs of Kingsland and Rutherford were riding in was hit by a three-inch round, which destroyed their automobile but left them unscathed. Fortunately, most of the shells in the plant had not yet been fitted with fuses, so they did not explode upon landing. Remarkably, not a single life was lost to the disaster.

The *Brooklyn Times Union* praised Tessie to the skies, asking, "Is there anything finer in the stories of nations than that? Isn't this telephone girl qualified to stand in glorious fame with the little Dutch boy who stopped the leak in the dike with his hand? Medals of gold and the honor of men for Tessie McNamara, the heroine of the Kingsland explosion! These, and all the happiness that can come to a girl, for she has deserved all of the good fortune that fate can bestow upon her."

Tessie's fame spread across the nation, in a month that saw the resumption of unrestricted submarine warfare by the Germans, making an American entry into the war almost an inevitability. The Concordia, Kansas *Blade-Empire* called "pretty and efficient" Tessie a "national heroine." Her courage was rewarded by "Mrs. William Alexander, president of The Special Aid Society," who sent her a twenty-five-dollar check "as a slight token of our appreciation of the splendid work you did in remaining at your post."

After the war, an international lawsuit, claiming that both Black Tom and Kingsland were the result of sabotage, was filed against Germany. In 1930, a German American Mixed Claims Commission decided against the United States and the lawsuit claimants, clearing Germany of any responsibility. Despite the decision, the claimants did not give up and continued to press their argument for sabotage.

In 1939, the Claims Commission met again to reconsider the case, this time without German participation. It ruled that the Germans had presented fraudulent information during the initial investigation and awarded $50 million to the American claimants. World War II intervened, and final arrangements for payment did not occur until a 1953 agreement with the Federal Republic of Germany (West Germany), which never admitted German responsibility but agreed to pay $50 million in damages to the claimants from both Black Tom and Kingsland explosions. Payment was finally made in 1979.

Tessie McNamara lived a quiet life after her actions in 1917. In 1930, she was working as a telephone operator in New York City and living with her sister's family at 715 Marian Avenue in Lyndhurst. She passed away on February 8, 1971, and was buried at St. Joseph's Cemetery in Lyndhurst. There is a memorial plaque to her at the scene of her heroism.

LEO P. GAFFNEY

A Slickster Banker

L eo P. Gaffney of Plainfield, New Jersey, seemed to have played the game right. By 1939, the New Jersey National Guardsman, a veteran of the Mexican border campaign and World War I who "had been cited for bravery in France," had risen from the rank of second lieutenant to lieutenant colonel in the Guard, where he served as an aide to New Jersey governor A. Harry Moore. Gaffney was no doubt politically involved, as it was common for the governor to appoint influential people in the National Guard to the position of aide, which automatically made them lieutenant colonels.

In the civilian sphere, Gaffney, a former Prohibition agent, had become the president of Bankers Industrial Service Inc., a Wall Street investment firm. But then there was an inquiry into "practices which the government alleges led to a $1,000,000 loss to investors." It turned out that Bankers Industrial Service, in which Gaffney and several other men had sold shares, had been, according to one investigator, "an empty shell." Gaffney and his fellow corporate officers were indicted for fraud by a federal grand jury in November 1939.

When the news broke, the Moore administration was quick to disown Gaffney. Although the governor himself did not make a statement, his office responded to a journalistic inquiry that while Gaffney was theoretically on the staff for more than a year, he had "reported for duty just once before being excused from further service" and that he "wore his staff uniform once, on the Decoration Day following his appointment."

Gaffney, who used about "$200,000 [$3,354,457 in today's money] of the corporation's funds in the purchase of a fifty-seven-foot yacht and other luxuries," and his associates were found guilty of mail fraud, violation of the Securities Exchange Act of 1933 (aka Glass-Steagall Act) and conspiracy. Gaffney, "the principal figure in the swindle," was sentenced to three and a half years in prison.

Although his wife remained active in affairs to benefit the Mount Carmel Guild charity, Gaffney disappears from New Jersey newspaper stories after his sentencing.

Leo P. Gaffney. *Author's collection.*

THERESA ANNA MARIA STABILE

"Dolly Dawn"

Theresa Anna Maria Stabile, daughter of a Montclair restaurant manager, was born in Newark, New Jersey, on February 3, 1916. After graduating from Montclair High School, she won first place and fifty dollars in a Newark amateur talent singing contest. In 1934, Stabile assumed the stage name Billie Starr and was singing with Frank Daily's Meadowbrook Syncopators, a band performing live shows every Tuesday, Wednesday and Friday on a CBS radio affiliate from Daily's Meadowbrook Club, a significant entertainment venue in Cedar Grove, New Jersey. Daily hired Billie because he was impressed with her "throaty tones, heard in praise of the 'blues' and things romantic."

After learning that New York City bandleader George Hall's female vocalist, Loretta Lee, was leaving his band, Billie arranged to audition for the slot, hoping that Hall, whose real name was George Pasillo, the judge of the talent contest she won, would remember her. She got the job, and when she and Hall were looking to come up with a new stage name for her, they settled on "Dolly Dawn." The story released about the name selection was that a Columbia University professor or an unidentified journalist (take your pick) who heard her sing told her, "You're as dimpled as a dolly, and as fresh as the dawn." A more reliable source attributed the quote to Harriet Mencken, a writer for the *New York Journal American*, who used the phrase in an interview with *Radio Guide* magazine. Soon Dolly Dawn was "hailed by many as the swingiest of swing songstresses and sweetest of torch singers" and was declared "one of the best girl singers radio has ever known." Interestingly,

Bandleader George Hall helps Dolly Dawn fix her hat in a 1937 publicity photo.
Author's collection.

Sheet music featuring Dolly and her "Dawn Patrol Boys." *Author's collection.*

every newspaper article about "Billie" or "Dolly" referred to her "real name" as Theresa Anna Maria Stabile, and one stated that longer names "simply don't fit on theater marquees, and that's why orchestra leaders as well as your favorite movie stars usually adopt shorter names." Of course, a desire to remove ethnicity may have been a factor as well.

Before hiring its Jersey girl, the George Hall Orchestra, which broadcast live six days a week from the Taft Hotel in New York City over CBS radio, had apparently been a popular but "uninspiring" dance band. A critic later noted that Dolly was "the one who gave it its zip." In the late 1930s, Hall began featuring Dawn with a small contingent of musicians, dubbing the group "Dolly Dawn and Her Dawn Patrol Boys." Her career took off, and she made a string of hit records, including "It's a Sin to Tell a Lie," "Every Minute of the Hour," "Robins and Roses," "Says My Heart," "My Own" and "Little Yellow Basket." She was voted "outstanding orchestra vocalist" for the year 1937, and her recording of "You're a Sweetheart" was the nation's number one song for a time in 1938.

Dolly Dawn was simultaneously under contract to two rival record labels: RCA with the George Hall Orchestra and Columbia as Dolly Dawn and Her Dawn Patrol Boys. Dolly and her "Patrol" made guest appearances on *Your Hit Parade* and the Bob Hope, Edgar Bergen and Milton Berle radio shows, and she developed a lifelong friendship with Ella Fitzgerald. In 1939, a newspaper declared that she was "one of the best of the country's popular singers."

When Hall decided to stop leading his band but still serve as its manager, he staged an elaborate ceremony on July 4, 1941, at New York's Roseland Ballroom, where he officially turned over the band's leadership to Dawn, who, according to several accounts, had been legally adopted by the bandleader and his wife at the age of nineteen. "It wasn't just a gimmick," a long-term friend later said. "When she took over the band, she actually learned to conduct." But in less than a year, as her musicians began to be drafted, like the "Boogie Woogie Bugle Boy of Company B," Dolly Dawn and Her Dawn Patrol Boys and the larger orchestra disbanded, and she pursued a solo career, although it never matched her previous successes. She "performed at clubs, dance halls and street fairs across the country." Interviewed in 1980, Dolly Dawn said, "I hated the name Dolly. It sounded like a stripper. All my friends call me Dawn— Dawn Stabile."

There was a Dolly Dawn revival of sorts in the 1980s, and she performed in several concerts that led to two new albums—*Smooth as Silk* and *Memories of You*—and appeared in New York clubs. *Los Angeles Times* jazz critic Leonard Feather described *Memories of You* as "one of the pleasant surprises of the season," marking "Dawn's reemergence as a first-rate, jazz-influenced singer." She had "developed a cult following which increased in recent years as some of her hits were reissued." Unfortunately, she, according to her relatives, received "almost no royalties" from her reissued work.

By the 1990s, Theresa Maria Stabile/Billie Starr/Dolly Dawn/Dawn Stabile was living in a "transient hotel" in Manhattan when the Actors Fund got her an apartment and, in her final years, moved her to the Fund's Nursing Home and Assisted Living Facility in Englewood, New Jersey. She died at the age of eighty-six on December 12, 2002, and was buried at the Actors Fund lot at Kensico Cemetery in Valhalla, Westchester County, New York.

We all agree that Theresa Anna Maria Stabile deserves a spot in the New Jersey Hall of Fame.

EUGENE H. VALLE

Colonel and Woman Chaser

Colonel Eugene H. Valle of Tenafly, New Jersey—who won first prize for the funniest costume at the Beaux Arts Costume Ball held at the British Colonial Hotel in Nassau, the Bahamas, in March 1936—liked to party.

Valle was born in Switzerland in 1888 and immigrated to America as a child. He joined the New Jersey National Guard as a private in June 1903 and had a long career both in the Guard and on active duty in the regular army, serving in the Mexican border campaign of 1916 as a lieutenant and then in World War I in the headquarters company of the 114th Infantry. He served in staff positions in World War II, including as a "plans and training officer" (S-3) at "a combat school in England where troops learn offensive and defensive street fighting" and later as an assistant inspector general. When not on active duty, Valle had a lucrative civilian career as a New York City diamond merchant.

Valle was a joiner and was a member of the Disabled American Veterans, Retired Officers Association, Veterans of Foreign Wars, American Legion, Reserve Officers Association and the 29th Division Association. He was also a Fourth Degree Knight of Columbus of Tenafly, a life member of the Tenafly Elks Lodge, an exempt fireman and a member of the New York 24 Carat Club, an association of diamond dealers.

Despite an apparently successful career, Valle did have his problems, and the newspapers made sure that everyone knew about them. In 1947, when he was living at 201 Crescent Parkway in Sea Girt, his wife, Teresa, hauled him into divorce court in Freehold, asking for "separate maintenance."

Colonel Valle at the Beaux Arts Ball. *Author's collection.*

She maintained that her husband, who had served on occupation duty in Germany for a year after the war, "boasted of his romantic conquests of German frauleins [especially one named Greta] and his extra-marital activities with a female government employee aboard a Continental luxury train in Germany." Teresa also maintained that the colonel had been "drunk and disorderly" and threatened her when he was home on leave during the war.

The Valles were back in court again in 1948, and the local newspapers eagerly followed the "battle of Valle vs. Valle." In lieu of paying his estranged wife the sixty dollars per month maintenance ordered by the court, the colonel had signed over the home on Crescent Parkway in Sea Girt to her and cleared up his call to police that there had been a $5,000 robbery at the house by disclosing that it was Mrs. Valle taking jewelry she claimed as her property.

At the final divorce hearing in Freehold on December 1, 1948, Teresa Valle elaborated on her husband's alleged offenses, claiming that while stationed at Fort Hamilton, New York, in 1943, he had "called her vile names in front of the commanding officer and other officers and their wives" and had been court-martialed in 1946 "for being disorderly on the Paris-Munich leave train."

Teresa went on to state that she "just had to learn to duck when Colonel Valle would hurl assorted household articles at her during rages," concluding that "that was one of his habits, to throw lamps, etc. He always tore my clothes off. If I put them down, he would destroy them."

Colonel Valle did not contest his wife's claims, and she was granted a divorce on grounds of "extreme cruelty." Valle retired from the army in 1949 and was living at the Albion Hotel in Asbury Park when he was honored with a dinner at the Fort Monmouth Officers' Club in June 1953. He died in 1964 and was buried at Arlington National Cemetery.

CARL BUEHLER

The War Bond Boy

Carl Buehler told folks that he wanted to "help see America is still free when I grow up." In October 1943, the ten-year-old Carl, a Verona, New Jersey resident, was a participant in his elementary school's war bond and stamp sale and accompanied his parents to a going-away party for a sailor at the Verona Inn. Carl used the occasion to make a "sales talk" and ended up selling $1,000 in bonds and $200 in stamps.

Buehler made the papers and assured a reporter that his campaign would continue and that he would "do something just as good, maybe better" in the future. He "appeared at rallies, on radio shows, and began a door-to-door campaign," pushing his patriotic product and raising his sales total to $5,450. At one rally, he was promised a ride in a jeep by an army officer, but the officer was overruled by his commander. Eager for the ride, Buehler went right to the top with his plea in a letter to President Franklin D. Roosevelt.

Although his family were Republicans, Buehler promised to vote for Roosevelt when he came of age. It no doubt appealed to the president's sense of humor, and it worked. Orders came down to give him his ride, and on November 10, 1943, a jeep showed up at Our Lady of the Lake School, where he was an honor student, and he rode off, as seen in the accompanying photo, to the cheers of his classmates. During the ride, Buehler leaned over and said to the driver, "Now about these war bonds. Could I sell you one?"

By the spring of 1944, Carl Buehler had sold $89,150 worth of war bonds, which, along with another letter to the president, earned him a ride in the

Carl Buehler on his jeep ride. *Author's collection.*

B-17 Flying Fortress "Hell's Angels." He told a reporter, "I wish I could have been flying over Berlin and dropping a few bombs."

Carl Buehler went on to move with his family to Manasquan, New Jersey, where he graduated from Manasquan High School in 1950 and then from Rutgers University; he served as a U.S. Marine Corps officer from 1954 to 1959. He then moved to Cherry Hill, where he founded a printing company and served as its CEO. Carl Buehler passed away at the age of sixty-eight in 2001.

JOHN BASILONE

New Jersey's Greatest Hero

B ack in the 1940s, the whole country knew who John Basilone was. He was the twenty-six-year-old heroic marine from Raritan, New Jersey, who had been awarded the Medal of Honor for his actions at Guadalcanal in 1942—the first marine to be awarded the medal during World War II. Today, he is still well known in his hometown, where he has a monument and is celebrated in an annual parade, as well as in surrounding towns in Somerset County and by military historians. Even though he was a leading character portrayed in the excellent HBO series *The Pacific*, he is largely forgotten by the general public in his native state and beyond.

An estimated total of 10,372 New Jerseyans, including 10 of the state's 17 Medal of Honor recipients, made the ultimate sacrifice and were killed in action or died of wounds or other causes during World War II. Marine Corps sergeant John Basilone was awarded the Medal of Honor for his heroic actions in defense of Henderson Field on Guadalcanal in 1942, where he held off a Japanese attack single handedly, hoisting a machine gun and firing it from the hip and then using his .45-caliber automatic pistol.

After a stint back in the United States on a tour selling war bonds with celebrities, which earned the government $1.4 million and included a stop at the Duke estate in Somerville, New Jersey, that drew thirty thousand people, Basilone, feeling twinges of guilt for abandoning his comrades, requested a return to combat duty and was killed in action after landing on Iwo Jima in February 1945, where his continued heroism earned him a Silver Star.

It did not take long for local veterans to commemorate Basilone's valor. In September 1945, the month the war officially ended, newly named

"Marine Congressional Medal of Honor Hero Sergeant John Basilone, USMC, of Raritan, NJ, recently visited the Marine Headquarters at Washington, D.C. Here, he is pictured telling Corporal Margaret Beerworth, USMCWR, some of his experiences on Guadalcanal." *Courtesy of USMC Archives.*

American Legion John Basilone Post 280 of Raritan proposed a new post building opposite the Basilone family home at 113 First Avenue in Raritan. The plan was for the building, complete with a "Basilone Memorial Room," to be situated in a small park, with a statue of the heroic marine standing out

Left: John Basilone at the time he received his Medal of Honor. *Author's collection.*

Right: The Orlando clay model of Basilone's statue. *Author's collection.*

front. Philip C. Orlando of Plainfield, New Jersey, an army veteran who had been awarded the Bronze Star while serving with the 9th Infantry Division in Europe and was a childhood friend of Basilone's and an accomplished sculptor, was contracted to create the "life sized figure in bronze."

Orlando completed the clay model for the statue in his Plainfield studio at 110 West Front Street in 1947, and it was sent to the Roman Bronze Works Inc., a foundry in Staten Island, to be cast into bronze. The statue was unveiled in Raritan on "Basilone Day," June 7, 1948, following a parade that included "uniformed Army and Marine troops, National Guardsmen, veterans' organizations, Boy Scouts, Girl Scouts, and numerous civil and fraternal groups." The ceremony was attended by "thousands of war veterans, distinguished public servants and townspeople," who turned out to honor Basilone. One newspaper estimated the total attendance at ten thousand people. The Camp Kilmer Army Band played the "Marine Corps Hymn," and then Mrs. Salvatore Basilone, the hero's mother, pulled a cord to unveil the statue. It stands to this day.

JOHN PARNELL FEENEY

A Slippery Politician

John Parnell Feeney was born into an Irish Catholic family in Jersey City, New Jersey, in 1895. Politically and economically ambitious from an early age, Feeney attended the University of Pennsylvania and served in the U.S. Army in World War I. In 1919, perhaps sensing the onset of an anti-immigrant and anti-Catholic era, sponsored in some part by the second iteration of the Ku Klux Klan, he reinvented himself as John Parnell Thomas, replacing his original last name with his mother's WASP-sounding maiden name; became an Episcopalian; and got a job working in the investment and insurance business in New York City.

In 1925, the former Mr. Feeney, by then known as "J. Parnell Thomas," was living in Allendale, New Jersey, where he became involved in local politics, serving as a councilman and mayor. A Republican, he was elected to the New Jersey State Assembly in 1935 and then to the U.S. Congress in 1936, an office to which he was reelected through 1948.

A staunch conservative, Thomas claimed that President Franklin D. Roosevelt was attempting to sabotage the capitalist system. As a member of the Dies Committee, named after its founder, Texas congressman Martin Dies, Thomas began to hunt alleged subversives, especially in the New Deal's Federal Theater Project, which he claimed promoted Communist propaganda. A contemporary noted that the congressman's "extraordinary zeal was tinged with a bitterness that bordered on fanaticism."

If anything, however, Thomas was focused on self-promotion. The late 1930s brought his attention to American Nazis and Virginia Cogswell, who had a brief career as a "slave trader" hostess in a bizarre attraction at Olympic Park. She said the Amusement Park's "Human Slave Market," the first of its kind, would "sell men and women to the highest bidder for matrimony." Tasteless even in the Depression, the enterprise was soon canceled, and then Cogswell was reportedly romantically involved with American Nazi leader Fritz Kuhn.

Cogswell was called before a New York federal grand jury investigating Kuhn's dubious fiscal activities with his organization's funds. Reporters flocked around the "plump Georgia peach and friend of the Fuhrer" as she arrived at the courthouse "wearing a becoming black hat and coat with a fur neckpiece." One journalist asked her if Kuhn "might properly be described as the great lover." Her response, with a smile, was, "Let us not go into that." She would later claim that she had been acting for the government in her relationship with Kuhn, although there is no evidence of that.

Cogswell was back in the news again in 1947, when columnist George Dixon interviewed Thomas and asked him about his role hunting Nazis for the Dies Committee. Thomas told Dixon, who had characterized Fritz Kuhn as "the hotsy-totsy Nazi," that "the lady-killing Kuhn was head over heels in love with Virginia many names," so called due to

Top: "The Georgia Peach," Virginia "many names" Cogswell. *Author's collection.*

Bottom: J. Parnell Thomas instructs the press. *Author's collection.*

her nine marriages, adding that when he and Cogswell were talking, he had an investigator enter the room and say, "We've got a line on Kuhn. He's got a very hot blonde out on Long Island."

According to Thomas, "The Georgia peach let out a screech as if she were hog calling all of her husbands. 'That dirty double-crossing Nazi rat!' she screamed. 'I'll show him and his blonde! I'll tell you where that two-timing skunk is hiding right now!'" Thomas claimed, "We accompanied her out to Long Island and grabbed Fritz Kuhn that night." This was a bold-faced lie on Thomas's part. Kuhn was arrested by New York detectives on an embezzlement charge in Krumsville, Pennsylvania, while on his way to Chicago.

Following the election of 1946, in which the Republicans gained the majority in Congress, Congressman Thomas became chairman of the House Unamerican Activities Committee, successor to the Dies Committee. With the Nazis a thing of the past, he expanded his previous search for left-wing subversives in the entertainment industry, traveling to Hollywood, where he met with film executives in 1947. Upon his return to Washington, he subpoenaed show business figures—including actors, directors, writers and musicians—to testify as to their supposed Communist connections before his committee. When some refused to testify, they were charged with and convicted of contempt of Congress. The congressman was riding high and eying an opportunity to run for vice president down the road.

Thomas's career was about to collapse, however. His secretary leaked correspondence to noted columnist Drew Pearson indicating that he demanded and received kickbacks from his staff and carried nonexistent employees on a padded payroll, pocketing the money himself. Thomas claimed that the stories were false and the result of "malice and political persecution," and he won reelection in 1948. When he appeared before a grand jury on the matter, Thomas responded like the Hollywood personalities he had condemned and refused to testify, citing, as they did, Fifth Amendment rights.

Congressman Thomas was indicted and tried on corruption charges. During the trial, he changed his original "not guilty" plea to "nolo contendre" and was fined $10,000 and sentenced to six to eighteen months in prison. He served nine months before he was pardoned by President Harry Truman. Several of Thomas's prison mates were, ironically, members of the "Hollywood Ten," sentenced for contempt of Congress.

Returning to Bergen County after his release, Thomas, who had paved the way for Senator Joe McCarthy's witch hunts and appointed Richard Nixon to the HUAC, adjusted poorly to a less important role in life. The congressman drank so heavily after his release that his wife, Amelia, divorced him and then remarried him several years later. He served as the publisher and editor of several Bergen County weekly newspapers and had publicity photos taken that portrayed him as a tough 1930s movie version of a reporter. He tried to return to Congress in 1954 but was defeated in the Republican primary. Thomas died in 1970 in St. Petersburg, Florida.

Thomas pretending to be a 1930s movie journalist. *Author's collection.*

In the 1990s, a reporter from the *Hackensack Record* interviewed Stiles Thomas, the congressman's son, who did not agree with any of his father's political views and maintained that he never spoke of politics with his father. Stiles's wife, Lillian, was upset because her father-in-law was not remembered as "the nice man I knew" before tearing up and said, "History will treat him more kindly." Stiles responded with, "I don't know. I don't know."

PELLEGRINO JAMES PELLECCHIA JR.

New Jersey's Best-Dressed Judge

Pellegrino James Pellecchia Jr., better known as P. James Pellecchia, was a Jerseyman on the rise in the late 1940s. His father had already risen from a five-dollar-per-week mason's helper to become a millionaire. Junior had done the exceptionally hard pre-natal work to be born into a future wealthy family in 1909, and over time, he became vice-president of his family-owned bank, Columbus Trust Company, as well as "chief boxing inspector" of the State of New Jersey. In 1946, Pellecchia, a Republican who held a law degree from George Washington University, became a magistrate in the Newark Police and Family Court, where he gained a reputation as "an uptight severe judge" who was especially hard on illegal gambling bookmakers. "Many foresaw a shining future," perhaps a slot on the New Jersey Supreme Court, for the jurist, a summer resident of Belmar who owned a luxurious home on Inlet Terrace and had once managed the Kingsley Arms hotel in Asbury Park.

Judge Pellecchia, aka "Judge Jimmy," made the news in January 1947 after ordering an investigation and the subsequent arrest of fifteen men involved in a sex trafficking "juvenile procurement ring," trading in "intimacies with teenagers." The judge described the case as "the most revolting in my history" and stated that it was the result of "lax parents and poor home conditions."

The judge was quite a dandy. In October 1947, the Fashion Foundation of America declared Pellecchia the country's "best dressed jurist." The organization stated that his "bright ties peeping from beneath his somber judicial robes" helped gain him the title. It was noted that "the brilliance

Pellegrino James Pellecchia Jr. leaving court after his conviction. *Author's collection.*

of Pellecchia's ties [he admitted to owning four hundred] gives his court new life." He also had a considerable wardrobe beyond his ties, including fifteen suits.

Suddenly things began to change, however. Pellecchia became far more lenient with bookies, even joking with them. Disreputable "hangers-on" were seen hanging in his courtroom. And then, in July 1948, he was arrested for embezzling $630,000 from Columbus Trust. The photo accompanying this section is of Pellecchia, sporting one of his fabled ties, as he left the court after confessing to the theft. Amid the evidence against him was a number of checks made out to the Iovine brothers, Newark bookmakers.

Pellecchia, redubbed the "Newark highflyer" by the press, revealed that he had gone through as much as $6,000 a week and, during one trip to Florida, $80,000, using "phony mortgages" as a source of the money. Where did the money go? Much of it was betting on horse races, but according to the Essex County prosecutor, "Pellecchia established little harems as it suited his convenience, not to mention his spending untold thousands on night life and other forms of luxurious living." Two of Pellecchia's "girl acquaintances" (there were many), who accompanied him to the track, New York model Gloria Cook and Toby Johnston, a dress designer from Caldwell, said they had no idea he was losing so much money.

Pellecchia had done his best to cover up the evidence of his malfeasance, but some assiduous investigating produced enough to convict him, and he pleaded guilty. The sentencing judge told Pellecchia that "he had done lasting damage to the judicial system." In January 1949, the fashionable jurist was sentenced to ten to fifteen years in prison for his fiscal crimes and sent to the State Prison Farm at Leesburg, New Jersey. His first stop on the incarceration trail was at the New Jersey State Prison, where a guard, "pointing to the bright orange and brown tie Pellecchia was wearing murmured: He won't be wearing them in here."

Denied parole in 1953, Pellecchia was paroled the following year due to a thyroid problem requiring surgery on the condition that he see a specialist. He was returned from the prison farm to Trenton, where he was released in his father's custody. A reporter noted that although Pellecchia was thinner than he was when he entered prison, he was still well attired, wearing "a light tan gabardine suit, brown and tan shoes and a dark tie."

Pellegrino James Pellecchia Jr. recovered from his illness and was married in 1956 to Michele Grenier, "an attractive blonde fashion stylist" he had met on the beach in Florida prior to his arrest. The couple honeymooned in France and then moved into an apartment in Montclair, where he lived for the rest of his life, which ended in 1985. At the time, the former judge was employed in his family's construction business—they kept him away from the bank.

ABNER "LONGIE" ZWILLMAN

Newark Gangster

It could reasonably be argued that, although he was generally accounted as a scoundrel, like many others of his type, Jewish gangster Abner "Longie" Zwillman had some admirable traits, most notably his mobilization of tough guys, or, as they were called in Yiddish, *shtarkers*, who knocked Nazis around on more than one occasion in Newark and its surrounding towns in the late 1930s. He had also offered a reward for the return of the kidnapped Lindbergh baby and donated $250,000 to a Newark slum clearance project during the Great Depression.

Zwillman was a guy who came up from nothing. Born in 1904, he had to quit school upon his father's death in 1918 and went into business selling groceries from a rented horse and wagon. A clever guy, Longie, so called because of his height, started selling "lottery" or "numbers racket" tickets when his grocery business did not do well. Like many sons of poor immigrants, he hopped on the bootleg bandwagon during Prohibition. It was the only route up the economic ladder for many. The money he made smuggling whiskey from Canada enabled him to expand his business model into the prostitution, gambling and labor rackets.

Longie—who also controlled, or at least heavily influenced, political activity in Newark in the 1930s—had his gang members steal and stuff ballot boxes to assure that Meyer C. Ellenstein, the first Jewish mayor in Newark history, would be elected and reelected during the decade. Zwillman was a high roller as well, hanging out with Joe DiMaggio, dating movie star Jean Harlow and buying her a red Cadillac and then marrying the daughter of a founder of the American Stock Exchange.

Above: Zwillman home in West Orange. *Author's collection.*

Right: Abner Zwillman in 1951. *Author's collection.*

In 1951, the Senator Estes Kefauver Senate Committee investigating organized crime examined Zwillman's operations. Longie, who temporarily disappeared to avoid appearing before the committee, eventually testified, admitting that he had been a bootlegger but claiming that all his post-Prohibition business had been legitimate. Much of it, however, was accomplished with laundered money, earned in enterprises like the gambling den he and Willie Moretti ran at the Riviera Club in Fort Lee.

Jules Endler, of Orange, New Jersey, was a Zwillman associate and owner of the Novelty Bar and Grill in Newark. He told the committee that Longie had used New York lawyer Arthur Garfield Hays, a well-known civil liberties attorney who had been on the defense team in the 1920s Scopes trial, as "a trustee" to invest his cash anonymously. Endler also noted that Longie had invested, often through Hays, in several Hollywood films, including *It's in the Bag*, starring Fred Allen, in 1944 and *Guest Wife*, starring Claudette Colbert, in 1945.

At the hearing, Jersey City mayor John V. Kenny denied that he knew Zwillman, although Charles Witkowski, Kenny's former public safety commissioner, claimed that he had been demoted because Kenny told him his anti-gambling crusade was "hurting our friends." In the end, Zwillman escaped from the investigation with nothing more than bad publicity.

In 1959, however, Senator John L. McClellan's Senate Committee investigating labor racketeering announced that it was going to subpoena Zwillman, but he was discovered hanging in the basement of his home at 50 Beverly Road in West Orange. Although Zwillman's death was ruled a suicide, many concluded that other mobsters had done him in, perhaps on the orders of Vito Genovese and Meyer Lansky.

RUTH CHENEY STREETER

Morristown's Marine Colonel

Ruth Cheney was born in Brookline, Massachusetts, in 1895. She was educated in a French boarding school and at Bryn Mawr college, graduating from the latter institution in 1917. In 1922, she and her husband, Thomas Streeter, an attorney and New York City bank officer, moved to Morristown, New Jersey. Streeter, who had four children, acquired a commercial pilot's license in 1942 and tried to join the Women Airforce Service Pilots (WASPs), ferrying planes to air corps bases. She was rejected as too old for the job but was offered a commission in the U.S. Marine Corps Women's Reserve in 1943.

Streeter was the first woman to become a major in the Marine Corps and went on to become the first director of the U.S. Marine Corps Women's Reserves. She retired in 1945 as a colonel and was active in postwar civic affairs, serving as a delegate to the New Jersey Constitutional Convention, which produced the third state constitution in 1947.

During the Cold War years of the 1950s, Mrs. Streeter was the director of Morristown's Civil Defense program. She was also involved in historic preservation efforts, particularly with Speedwell Village, and was secretary of the nonprofit organization dedicated to preserving that site, the location of the first successful telegraph message. Her dedication led to Governor Richard Hughes appointing her to the New Jersey Historic Sites Commission. She made significant contributions to her adopted state.

One of the photos accompanying this story is of Colonel Streeter reviewing a parade of female marines on the first anniversary of the

Left: Colonel Streeter reviewing a parade of female marines in February 1944. Standing alongside her is Eleanor Roosevelt and Marine Corps commandant Lieutenant General A.A. Vandegrift. *Author's collection.*

Right: Ruth Cheney Streeter cutting a ribbon in a local dedication in May 1969. *Author's collection.*

founding of the Marine Corps' Women's Reserve in February 1944. Standing alongside her is Eleanor Roosevelt and Marine Corps commandant Lieutenant General A.A. Vandegrift. The second photo is of Ruth Cheney Streeter cutting a ribbon in a local dedication in May 1969. She passed away in 1990, after dedicating a lifetime to her state and country.

JOHN HVASTA

Iron Curtain Escape Artist

February 6, 1954, was probably one of the most illustrious days in the history of Hillside, a suburb of Newark with some twenty-five thousand residents. It was the day John Hvasta came home.

Hvasta's return was no ordinary occasion. The twenty-six-year-old man was reuniting with his parents and brother after five bitter years of imprisonment in what was described as "a filthy Middle Ages dungeon" and subsequently dodging Communist police in Czechoslovakia following a daring escape.

Arriving at New York's Idlewood Airport (today's JFK Airport), an emotional Hvasta fell into the arms of his mother and murmured, "Thank God, thank God." Hvasta was whisked to New Jersey for an enormous homecoming celebration, where he told a cheering crowd, "I always kept my faith in the American people and my faith in God. Had I lost that faith, I would have lost myself."

Certainly, a strong measure of faith was a critical factor in Hvasta's abilities to withstand the harrowing ordeal that began when he was accused of espionage while working as an interpreter at the U.S. Consulate in Bratislava, Czechoslovakia.

Hvasta, a naturalized U.S. citizen who was born in Czechoslovakia and spoke fluent Slovak, had returned to that country from the United States to study philosophy. At the time, the country was in the throes of a political struggle that ended with the Communist party seizing control and forming an alliance with the Soviet Union.

A victim of the political paranoia gripping the country, Hvasta was arrested in October 1948 and charged with espionage. Despite requests from the American Embassy in Prague to release Hvasta, he was tried by a secret court in June 1949 and sentenced to three years in prison, a term extended by an additional ten years in 1950. Hvasta was confined to a dungeon-like cell in Leopoldov.

American officials continued to work for his release, and New Jersey congressman Peter Rodino took an intense interest in the case, as did the New Jersey VFW.

In January 1952, Hvasta made a daring escape with five other inmates and then disappeared. In 1953, he was reported as recaptured, but the Czechoslovakian government refused to confirm or deny the story. When American sanctions produced the release of confined Associate Press reporter James Oatis, Congressman Rodino demanded and secured a personal meeting with President Eisenhower concerning "forgotten man" John Hvasta. Eisenhower was impressed with Rodino's presentation and immediately asked Secretary of State John Foster Dulles to make every effort to bring Hvasta home.

Media coverage reflected the public's preoccupation with the case. "The question is: Where is John Hvasta?" queried the *Pittsburgh Press* in its June 1, 1953 edition. The Czech government's refusal to confirm or deny the report that Hvasta had been recaptured following his prison escape was torturous for his parents, who were "denied even the small mercy of knowing either that their son is back in prison or at large somewhere behind the Iron Curtain."

"Well, it is time the State Department became a little more insistent about the case of John Hvasta, American citizen," the news story continued. "It should call in the Czech ambassador and tell him we want to know immediately where John Hvasta is—if he is in prison or at large, if he is dead or alive."

Hvasta was indeed alive and still at large following his prison escape. He was living in the Czech countryside, "hiding in haystacks and caves" and aided by "generous country folk." On October 2, 1953, he appeared at the U.S. Embassy in Prague, where he was granted refuge. Under pressure from Dulles, the Czech government allowed him to leave the country, accompanied by diplomats, on February 4, 1954.

Days later, an undoubtedly overwhelmed Hvasta was back in his hometown, greeted by throngs of well-wishers. The Hillside High School drum and bugle corps led a mile-long parade to Hvasta's modest two-family home. Fire engines

John Hvasta waves from an automobile in his homecoming parade. *Author's collection.*

in the procession blared their horns while children ran alongside Hvasta's car screaming, "Welcome home, Johnny." A physical reminder of Communist oppression in Czechoslovakia was in the parade: the homemade tank in which eight Czechs crashed through the Iron Curtain in 1952.

Hvasta's parents, observed one reporter, "appeared bewildered by the confusion and wanted only to be alone with the son they hadn't seen in five years." Simmering on the stove in Mrs. Hvasta's "spic and span" kitchen was a big pot of chicken noodle soup, Czechoslovakian style, Hvasta's favorite.

Milton Conford, a former Hillside mayor, paid tribute to Hvasta's "beautiful, lovely, patient mother, who has been given God's greatest blessing—a return of her son."

Hvasta's homecoming was especially meaningful to Juraj Slavik, a former Czech ambassador, now in exile, whose son was in the same prison from which Hvasta escaped. "I am as happy today as if my own son were in this free country," Slavik said.

For Hvasta, his jubilant homecoming was the beginning of a successful readjustment to life as a free man after years of stress and deprivation.

Following his return, Hvasta embarked on a public speaking tour, graduated from the University of Southern California with a degree in cinematography and then worked as a freelance documentary filmmaker. He later moved to Washington, D.C., formed a public relations company and worked on the Eisenhower reelection campaign and, subsequently, the campaigns of Richard Nixon and Ronald Reagan.

With the fall of Communism, Hvasta made a triumphant return to Slovakia, where he was interviewed on radio and television. Hvasta retired in 1999 and died in Florida in 2013.

All those accomplishments were unknown possibilities on that joyous day in 1954, when Hvasta was engulfed in the warm embrace of his friends and family in Hillside. He was undoubtedly both exhilarated and exhausted when he gave his final comments of the day to a cluster of news-hungry reporters on the steps of his humble home. "First of all," he said, "I'd like to thank all of you fine people for the wonderful welcome you have given me. It really makes a person glad to be home." Hvasta talked a bit more about his faith in his adopted country.

Then he smiled, waved his key to the township and an American flag in the air and went into his house to be alone with his family.

BIBLIOGRAPHY

Books

Adelberg, Michael S. *The American Revolution in Monmouth County: The Theatre of Spoil and Destruction.* Charleston, SC: The History Press, 2010.

Adelberg, Michael S., and Harry Ziegler. *Asbury Park: A Brief History.* Charleston, SC: The History Press, 2009.

Bilby, Joseph G. *"Freedom to All": New Jersey's African-American Civil War Soldiers.* Hightstown, NJ: Longstreet House, 2011.

———. *New Jersey: A Military History.* Yardley, PA: Westholme, 2017.

Bilby, Joseph G., ed. *New Jersey Goes to War: Biographies of 150 New Jerseyans Caught Up in the Struggle of the Civil War, Including Soldiers, Civilians, Men, Women, Heroes, Scoundrels—and a Heroic Horse.* Hightstown, NJ: Longstreet House, 2010.

Bilby, Joseph G., and Harry Ziegler. *The Rise and Fall of the Ku Klux Klan in New Jersey.* Charleston, SC: The History Press, 2010.

Bilby, Joseph G., and Katherine Bilby Jenkins. *Monmouth Court House: The Battle that Made the American Army.* Yardley, PA: Westholme Publishing, 2010.

Cumming, John. *Runners and Walkers: A Nineteenth Century Sports Chronicle.* Chicago: Regnery Publishing, n.d.

Cunningham, John T. *New Jersey, America's Maim Road.* Garden City, NY: Doubleday, 1966.

Federal Writers' Project. *New Jersey: A Guide to Its Present and Past.* New York: Viking Press, 1939.

———. *Stories of New Jersey, Its Significant People, Places and Activities*. New York: M. Barrows & Company, 1938.

Fleming, Thomas. *New Jersey, a Bicentennial History*. New York: Norton, 1977.

Fox, Thomas. *Drummer Boy Willie Magee, Civil War Hero and Fraud*. New York: McFarland, 2019.

Getz, William. *Sam Patch: Ballad of a Jumping Man*. Chicago: Regnery Gateway Publishing, 1981.

Jameson, Wallace. *Religion in New Jersey: A Brief History*. New York: Van Nostrand, 1964.

Lucas, Richard. *Axis Sally: The American Voice of Nazi Germany*. Philadelphia, PA: Casemate Publishing, 2013.

Lurie, Maxine, and Marc Mappen, eds. *Encyclopedia of New Jersey*. New Brunswick, NJ: Rutgers University Press, 2004.

Lurie, Maxine, and Richard Veit, eds. *New Jersey: A History of the Garden State*. New Brunswick, NJ: Rutgers University Press, 2012.

Mappen, Marc. *Jerseyana: The Underside of New Jersey History*. New Brunswick, NJ: Rutgers University Press, 1994.

———. *There's More to New Jersey than the Sopranos*. New Brunswick, NJ: Rivergate Press, 2009.

Reddan, William. *Other Men's Lives: Experiences of a Doughboy, 1917–1919*. Yardley, PA: Westholme Publishing, 2017.

Reisinger, John. *Master Detective: The Life and Crimes of Ellis Parker, America's Sherlock Holmes*. N.p.: Glyphworks Publishing, 2012.

Scull, Andrew. *Madhouse: A Tragic Tale of Megalomania and Modern Medicine*. New Haven, CT: Yale University Press, 2005.

Newspapers

Allentown (NJ) Messenger
Baton Rouge Tri-Weekly Advocate
Blade-Empire (Concordia, Kansas)
Brooklyn (NY) Citizen
Brooklyn Daily Eagle
Burlington (NJ) Courier News
Columbia (SC) State
Courier Post (Camden)
Fort Worth Star Telegram
Hackensack Record

Home News (Central New Jersey)
Jackson (NJ) Sun
Los Angeles Times
Minneapolis Star Tribune
Monmouth Democrat
Morristown (NJ) Daily Record
Newark Advertiser
New York Clipper
New York Journal American
New York Times
Paterson (NJ) Daily News
Pittsburgh Press
Trenton Evening Times

ABOUT THE AUTHORS

JOSEPH G. BILBY received his BA and MA degrees in history from Seton Hall University. He served as a lieutenant in the 1st Infantry Division in Vietnam, retired as an investigations supervisor from the New Jersey Department of Labor and is now part-time assistant curator of the National Guard Militia Museum of New Jersey in Sea Girt. He is the author, coauthor or editor of twenty-two books, two of which are on the New Jersey State Historical Commission's list of "101 Great New Jersey Books," and he's a freelance writer and historical consultant. He served on the New Jersey Civil War Sesquicentennial Committee and was editor of several of its publications, including the award-winning *New Jersey Goes to War*, a book on 150 of the state's Civil War–era personalities; *A History of Submarine Warfare Along the Jersey Shore*; *New Jersey: A Military History*, which covers the military story of the Garden State from 1607 to the present; and *The Rise and Fall of the Ku Klux Klan in New Jersey*. Mr. Bilby has been awarded the Jane Clayton Award for contributions to Monmouth County (New Jersey) history, an Award of Merit from the New Jersey Historical Commission for his contributions to the state's military history and the prestigious Richard J. Hughes Prize from the state's historical commission for his work.

HARRY ZIEGLER received his BA degree from Monmouth University and his MA degree from Georgian Court University. He rose from reporter to managing editor of the *Asbury Park Press* before leaving to pursue a second career in education and is now principal of St. Thomas Aquinas High School in Edison, New Jersey. He has coauthored eight books on New Jersey history with Joseph Bilby.

6/25/2024